Praise

Working Parents **Happy Kids**

"The anxiety of separation begins with the infant's first game of peek-a-boo and never leaves us. *Working Parents, Happy Kids* is loaded with ideas to help ease the pain of separation: ranging from the parent as video star right down to the humble penciled note in the child's lunch box."

—JACKIE SPARROW, PRE-SCHOOL EDUCATOR FOR 27 YEARS,
ST. MARY'S CREATIVE PLAYSCHOOL

"*Working Parents, Happy Kids* is a wonderful "how-to" book on an incredibly important issue for parents—how to find creative ways to stay in touch with their children emotionally and physically while working. As a marriage and family therapist, I highly recommend this book to every working parent."

—KATY BARLOON, M.A., L.M.F.T.

"The Mothers' Support Network is supportive of anything that enhances relationships between parents and their children. *Working Parents, Happy Kids* really delivers on its promise to help parents and children stay connected during working hours."

—LAURA WESTRUP, MOTHERS' SUPPORT NETWORK, SACRAMENTO, CA

"A great book filled with numerous ways to stay close to your child, both at home and away. Many children of traveling parents experience abandonment issues, and the use of the material in this work will go a long way in terms of prevention."

—JOEL WIEMAN, PH.D., FAMILY THERAPIST

"What a great book! *Working Parents, Happy Kids* is chock full of creative ideas on how to bridge the distance—between cities or city blocks—to stay connected with our kids as they grow and change."

—PAM CRAVEZ, COLUMNIST, ALASKA PARENTING MAGAZINE

"If you buy only one parenting book this year, it should be *Working Parents, Happy Kids*. The activities in this book enable families to celebrate their unity—even while physically separated."

—JENNY ORTON, 4TH GRADE TEACHER, HUFFMAN ELEMENTARY SCHOOL

"A long-overdue, much needed tool for working parents. The information and suggestions are priceless."

—LOURDES MARIA MONSERRAT, M.A., J.D.,
OPERATOR OF HEADSTART PROGRAMS IN HONDURAS

"An excellent work, offering a plethora of unique strategies for all families experiencing separations of days, weeks or simply hours duration. I will be recommending it to my clients, my friends and to my husband!"

—LINDA CERRO, ESQ., FAMILY LAW ATTORNEY, MOTHER OF TWO

Working Parents **Happy Kids**

STRATEGIES FOR STAYING CONNECTED

Pati Crofut
Joanna Knapp

Published by:
Turnagain Press
P.O. Box 240248
Anchorage, AK 99524-0248 U.S.A.
Fax: 907-248-3623
E-mail: turnagain@ibm.net

Edited by: Robin Quinn
Cover Design: Irving Freeman
Interior Design and Layout: Cara Showers and Diane Scott
Indexed by: Katrina Lemke

Printed in the United States of America

ISBN: 0-9663499-8-9
Library of Congress Catalog Card Number: 97-65432

Publisher's Cataloging-in-Publication
Crofut, Pati.
    Working parents, happy kids : strategies for staying
connected / Pati Crofut and Joanna Knapp. — 1st ed.
    p. cm.
    Includes index.
    ISBN: 0-9663499-8-9

    1. Working mothers--Life skills guides. 2. Parents—Life
skills guides. 3. Children of working parents—Psychology.
4. Parent and child. 5. Work and Family. I. Knapp, Joanna.
II. Title.

HQ759.48.C76 1998   646.7'0085
                             QBI98-381

ACKNOWLEDGMENTS

Any project that has undergone as many changes as this one will have lots of people to acknowledge for their contributions. Since this book started out as **The Travel Tracker**, our thanks go to all those involved in its birth and its subsequent reincarnation as **Working Parents, Happy Kids.** The following people deserve special acknowledgment:

Roger Davis—who took the time and the energy to help us see this book was hiding in **The Travel Tracker.**

Leigh Whitaker—who broached the idea of listing children's books and came up with many titles off the top of her head.

Tracy Stewart—who gave us a real boost of confidence by using some of the ideas in the book with her own child, and who encouraged us to find more books for our youngest audience.

Sally Tilton—who gave us a perfectly beautiful drawing for the cover of **The Travel Tracker**.

George Mason—who told us that this was a book before we were willing to believe it.

Kim Olmstead, Linda Longstaff, Janice Weiss and Liz Johnson—who took the time and energy from their busy schedules to read and critique this book.

Dana Stabenow—who kept telling us to quit talking about it and write!

Robin Quinn—who led us through the editing process step-by-step and pointed us in the right direction for help when we needed it.

Dan Poynter—who illuminated every step of the publishing process and is still lighting the way.

The families whose quotes appear in the book—our thanks go to them for letting us ask all kinds of questions, and for not being afraid to have their lives made public.

Jim Lavrakas—who, with the help of his trusted assistant, invested the time and patience needed to capture a warm, happy photograph of all of us.

Tracy Green—for coming up with this wonderful title.

Terrie Gottstein—for her input on the holidays and her insights in general.

Pati wishes to dedicate her effort in this book to her mother, Carmel Crofut, to her two children, and to the memory of her daughter, Danny. She also wishes to thank the Federal Express pilot who provided the absences; Catherine Call, Danny Lee, Pat Whelan, Don Kelly, Lourdes Monserrat, Lizette Stiehr, Beth Pope and Joanna Knapp for encouraging and inspiring her journey; and God, for the daily inner guidance and peace.

Joanna would like to thank her husband, David, for encouraging her to pursue her dreams and whose support has made it all possible; her mother, Polly, for being a wonderful role model and friend; and her father, Bill, for teaching her always to embrace a challenge. She would also like to thank Catherine Call, Laura Westrup, Caroline Rodgers, and Vicki Novak—who patiently listened while this book unfolded—and Pati Crofut, who helps make writing and publishing books a joy. Finally, she would like to thank Kristin, who has shown her how great a daughter can be, and Alex and Ian—her happy kids—who make it all worthwhile.

CONTENTS

PREFACE

Initially, the purpose of this book was to offer families ways to ease the stress of business travel. As mothers of young children and wives of traveling husbands, we knew about it first hand. We lived with the difficulties of single parenting when our husbands were gone, and we endured answering "When is Daddy coming home?" for the twentieth time in one day. More importantly, we observed a helplessness in our children and the traveling parent as they separated and lost contact with each other. Our response was to create ways for letting our young children know where their Daddy was, what he was doing, and when he was coming home. We devised methods for both of them to remain connected with each other throughout the trip.

As time went on, our lives changed, and so did the scope of this book. Our children got older, and new separations arose. Our own work, our children's schooling and activities, family illnesses and divorce gave us a whole new set of challenges. Schedules became vastly more complicated, and our family members' time away from each other increased. It became evident that everyone involved—the children, the absent parent and the parent or caregiver at home—had their own unique set of issues to handle. We soon realized that our techniques and strategies for travel could be expanded to help our families remain connected in the face of any kind of separation.

And so, as our families' needs changed, our strategies did too. For the days when we were all scattered to the four winds, we devised dozens of methods of communicating using just about every form except smoke signals. When evening meetings kept us away from home, we found ways to leave touches of our love at dinner and at the homework table. We created techniques to combat the pain and disappointment of missing a special event, or of not being there when our children were sick. And as we added additional activities and techniques to our own families' repertoires, that in turn became part of this book.

After writing about the ideas and activities that worked for us, we shared them with our friends who offered us their own tips in return. We then passed the manuscript around to several families for thorough critiques. The wisdom of all these friends and acquaintances appears in quotations throughout the text. Next, we consulted a social worker and a psychologist, who both specialize in children ages two to twelve. They analyzed the activities to determine if they were age-appropriate and psychologically sound. And now, we present it all to you.

Our wish is that you will pick and choose what your family needs. It is our hope that these activities will give your family wonderful memories, strong connections to each other, and a springboard for the birth of your own strategies. Our goal is that you will be able to walk out your front door with a little less guilt, and that your children will understand and accept the inevitable separations of life. Finally, we hope that you learn, like we have, that you can't do it all. You won't always pick the right thing to do or say, but in spite of the hectic pace in all our lives, you can help keep your family's heart strings connected and reverberating to the loving strains of your family's music.

—Pati and Joanna

1
GETTING STARTED

Parents are going to be absent. Nobody can be there constantly, and that is not the goal either. It is not the absence so much as how the child perceives the absence. That's where parenting comes in. The parent's job is to help their child perceive and integrate those absences. If it is a good absence, the child will receive increased self-worth, increased self-reliance, a sense of safety in the world, and a more developed sense of staying connected. They will understand that you don't need to be holding a hand to remain connected, that you don't need to be in the same room, that there is always a psychic connection, a spiritual connection, a family connection that transcends the physical.
— *Richard Kurtz, M.P.H., M.A. Counseling Psychology, L.M.F.T.*

Separations are a fact of life. If you are like most Americans, you are a working parent who spends time away from your family. You and your children probably go in different directions each workday. In addition to these regular absences, you may work overtime, travel for business, or have outside activities that draw you away from your children. Even stay-at-home parents experience separations from their children.

Some days, leaving your children proceeds without a hitch. Hugs and kisses and choruses of "See you later!" mark most of your routine goodbyes. But sometimes your customary routine hits a snag. Your child becomes needy and clinging. Goodbyes that were a breeze last week have now become difficult.

Even when the goodbyes are smooth, we *all* have concerns about separations from our children—especially if they are young. When we are away from our children, we wonder if they are safe, well cared for, and happy. Our children also have concerns about our separations. Noted among their questions are: "Where are you going?" "Can I go with you?" "When are you coming home?" "Who will take care of me?" and "When *will* I get to spend time with you?"

This book is about separations. It is for the parent with children between the ages of two and twelve. This book will help both you and your children ease any anxiety you have about leaving each other. There is *no* substitute for the precious time spent with your children, and that is not what this book is about. Instead, it is about making the inevitable separations your family faces easier and happier for all of you.

This book shows you how to answer your child's questions about your absences in a way that helps them feel safe, secure and well-loved. It also helps you develop a grab bag of activities and strategies specifically tailored to your child that can be used whenever your child needs extra reassurance of your love. You can't be in two places at once, but your love can be. This book will help you show your children that you love and care about them—even while you are at work.

DO I HAVE THE TIME TO DO THIS?

Whenever I have something I want busy people to read, I tell them to put it in the bathroom. If they can grab a few minutes here or there, they'll have it read before they know it. This is a really good bathroom book. You can look through and pick out activities in just a few minutes. You can mark them and then go back to them when you want to later.

—Heidi

You do have the time if you have only one hour a week. And what does an hour of your time amount to? One less TV show? An extra ten minutes of reading every night? Spending one lunch hour reading this instead of performing your usual routine? It won't be easy, but that kind of time is there.

We've all bought those parenting books that tell us step-by-step how to get our house and family running like a finely tuned Ferrari. If we find the time to read the book in the first place, we pour over a few relevant chapters and—filled with enthusiasm—launch into a head-on attack. After a week or two, we are exhausted and everything starts to unravel. How many of us actually make it past Week Three? Our failure to follow these plans has nothing to do with our willingness to solve the problem or our execution of the book's instructions. It all boils down to lack of time and energy.

You and your family's lives are probably crammed to the gills already. When either Mom or Dad tries to institute a whole new system, everyone gets frustrated. Imagine instead introducing *only one* new change each week or two. It's tempting to jump in and try it all this very week, but DON'T! Tackling one problem area at a time will help you sail past Week Three.

So start today, but start slowly. Use your hour this week to start reading the book. Study the strategy given below for getting started. After a week or two of reading, pick an activity to try during the next week. You will be spreading your loving touch before you know it. It can work if you take it slowly.

HOW TO USE THIS BOOK—
EASY DOES IT

Any good organizational tool comes with a game plan, and this book is no different. The key is to relax and start slowly.

- Start by reading through the chapters called **Answering the Questions All Children Ask** on pages 17-28 and **Building the Lines of Communication** on pages 29-58.

- Next, look through the Table of Contents and pick an area where you think your children could use more attention from you.

- Read the chapter or section covering that area. If there are any references to other chapters, look through them if they pertain to your problem.

- Pick an initial activity that you think your child might like.

- Prepare this activity so that either you or the adult at home can implement it at the appropriate time.

- Evaluate the activity after it has been tried. Ask your children. Ask your caregiver. Watch and listen.

- Decide to stick with the activity or select another one to replace it.

- Try one new activity per week in that same area of concern until you have found your family's favorites.

- Start on a new area.

There are a lot of activities in this book, and we don't expect your family to use them all. The reason for trying some of these strategies is to make your life easier and to reassure your child of your love. So get started, but remember to be gentle on yourself. You cannot do and be everything for your family—not even with all the books and activities in the world at your disposal. Remember, you are only human, and just by trying, you have already proven yourself a loving, caring parent.

2
ANSWERING THE QUESTIONS ALL CHILDREN ASK

Maybe it is because I work out of my home, or due to the fact that I don't have a regular routine, but it seems that I am always answering questions from my children about when I will be home and where I am going. They really have a need to know what I am doing beyond the bounds of curiosity. If they have all the pieces of the puzzle in place, if they can picture me where I am going, my leaving seems to be easier for them to accept.

—Joanna

When you leave your children, it often seems to them as if you disappear into a black hole only to be deposited back at your home hours or—in the case of a business trip—days later. From your children's point of view, their contact with you is abruptly severed. In young children, fears, anxiety and concern over your well-being can result from their inability to imagine where you are and what you are doing. How can your children have a good time while you are gone if they don't understand the basics of why you leave in the first place? If you take the time to make sure they have a sense of where you are going, why you have to go there, and when you are coming home, it can take away all the mystery of your departure.

Before you leave, whether it is for an hour or a week, children usually want to know the same things: "Why do you have to go?" "Where are you going?" "Why can't I go with you?" "When are you coming home?"

and "Who will take care of me while you are gone?" In each case, they may be merely asking for information, or they may be truly concerned about some aspect of your leaving. It's best to always treat your children's questions seriously and answer them thoughtfully. Start out by answering the actual question they asked in a simple direct manner. Don't let your concerns prompt you into babbling long and involved answers they may not either want or be ready for. Next, determine what they actually heard from you and help them understand your answer as best you can.

WHY DO YOU HAVE TO GO?

In most American homes, both parents or the single parent work. Our children grow up with their parent(s) leaving for work as a natural part of their lives. Occasionally, the question "Why do you have to go?" will crop up. Most often, when your children ask this question, they simply want to know why you can't hang out with them that particular day. They are thinking that it would be more fun for them to stay home with you than to go to school or daycare. Sometimes when they ask this question, however, there is more to it. Maybe there is something troubling them about their daycare situation or they are feeling needy for other reasons. How can you find out?

When I want to get information from my children, I try to ask it in a way that they won't know the purpose of the question. If they think I am apprehensive about their school or daycare environment, they tend to play on those emotions so maybe they can stay with me instead.
—Mary

Questions to Ask Your Child

- How are you feeling about my leaving for work? Is there something special about today that makes you want me to stay home?

- If there were something you could change related to your school/daycare, what would it be?
  Possibilities:
  - Homework not completed
  - Problems with peers—a bully, a friend who is ignoring them
  - Bathroom problems with very young children

- Do you need me to do anything special for you today?
  Suggestions:
  - Offer them a keepsake to take with them for the day.
  - Ask if they want you to call them during the day.
  - Inform the adult with them during the day that your child needs extra hugs today.
  - Set a time to sit down together and figure out a solution to their problem.

Sometimes your children simply wonder why you go to work at all. Why *do* you leave them day after day? This can be especially true if you have just recently returned to work, made a job change, or started traveling. Your child may not understand why you have to be gone more than before. Answer these questions for yourself first.

Why *Am* I Going to Work?

- Why do I work?
  Possible Answers:
  - Because I enjoy my job.
  - Because my family needs the money.
  - Because my job makes a contribution to society.
  - Because I like the balance it gives my life.
  Your Answer: Because_____

- What do I like about my job?
  Possible Answers:
  - I like the people I work with.
  - I like what I do.
  - I like what we can buy with the money.
  Your Answer:_____

- What benefits does my job provide my family?
  Possible Answers:
  - Our home and food
  - Health insurance
  - Vacation money
  - Lessons and after-school activities
  Your Answer: _____

- If you travel, what do you like about your business travel?
  Possible Answers:
  - Time away from my family rejuvenates me.
  - It helps me appreciate my family more.
  - It allows me time to get to know my co-workers.
  - It gives me a chance to get a lot of work done.
  - It gives me a chance to see new places.
  Your Answer: _____

Books for Young Children
The Terrible Thing That Happened At Our House by Marge Blaine
Sonya's Mommy Works by Arlene Alda
My Mommy Makes Money by Joyce Slayton Mitchell
Meredith's Mother Takes the Train by Deborah Lee Rose
The Trouble With Dad by Babbette Cole
Both My Parents Work by Katherine Leiner
The Berenstain Bears and Mama's New Job by Stan Berenstain

Put your answers into words that your children will understand. If you truly like your job, you are lucky. Your list of reasons will be long. If you do not like your job, focus on the personal and family benefits you just came up with. You want to steer clear of telling your children that you hate your job unless you are in the process of making a positive change. If this is the case, and your child is older, by all means bring them in on that process. Tell them you have identified a problem in your life. Share with them the possible solutions that are available to you and demonstrate how you will take action.

WHERE ARE YOU GOING?

I am a flight attendant, and I've taken the kids to stay in the hotel where I layover in Seattle. I even took both my daughters to work with me on the "Take Your Daughter to Work" day. They worked the flight right along with me. We went to Bethel and they wore sweaters that are part of the uniform and they collected trash, cups and things. The logistics were hard to iron out, but it worked wonderfully. That day they really learned what I do at work!

—Jan

Most children—especially younger ones—want to know where you are going and what you will be doing while you are there. Even if you have been talking about your meeting or trip for days, it is important to take the time to sit down and explain to your children where you will be while you are gone. The whole idea is to help them form an accurate picture in their mind of where you will be after you disappear from them.

I work in the oil field in northern Alaska. I work seven days on, then have seven days off. Every other week, my children watched me get on an airplane and head out for parts unknown. When I showed my eight-year-old daughter pictures of where I slept when I went away for work, it was important to her. She said, "Wow, you don't live in a house up there! I always wondered where you lived."

—Candi

Showing Children Where You Are Going and What You Will Be Doing When You Get There

- If You Will Be at Work or Somewhere Locally:
- At some point, give your kids a complete tour of your workplace. Show them what you do during a day—not only where you work but also where you eat lunch or hang out.
- If you are starting a class or some activity that will be new to you, give your children a drive-by. Take your family for a ride and show them where you are going to be. If you can, take them inside also. End the outing with a visit to the park or an ice cream cone to plant a favorable impression of your absence in their mind. After you have started your activity, tell them how it is going. Tell them about the teacher and how you are doing in class. Give them a laugh by telling them about any funny things that have happened in class.

- If You Are Going to Be Out-of-Town:
  - Use a map to show your children where you are going.
  - Give older children any itineraries, travel brochures or any other written information pertaining to your absence. Anything with pictures will work for younger children.
  - Ask the hotel to fax or mail you brochures or postcards.
  - If your travel is going to be extensive, take a field trip to the library or surf the Internet for information about your destination.
  - Talk about what you will do when you get there—what meetings you will attend and if it is going to be just a few people or a large conference.

I miss my kids the most when I am on a trip and I can't picture what they are doing. If they are in their usual routine, I know where they are and what they are doing just about every hour of the day. When I am gone and they are at their dad's, I just can't develop a picture of where they are, and I seem to miss them all the more. It helps me to know what they are doing just as much as it helps them to know what I am doing.

—Jan

Why Can't I Go with You?

I would regularly take my children to work with me for an hour or two on the weekends. They played games on a spare PC or I brought things to keep them busy. They also got a soda and a candy bar. Therefore, they loved coming with me for short periods of time. It served two purposes. They became very familiar with my workplace, so they could then picture where I was and what I was doing when I worked. It also helped curb the question of coming with me. They realized that coming with me for more than a short time was pretty boring!

—Mary

It's perfectly natural for young children to want to go with you—especially if they are sad about your leaving. In their minds, going along presents a perfect solution to the problem of your impending absence. They reason that if they go with you, you can get your work done and be with them at the same time. You need to gently let them know why their company is not appropriate right now.

You Can't Go with Me Because . . .

- Equate your work with something in their lives that they do without you, such as play with a friend or attend preschool. Tell them that you don't attend preschool with them because the classes are just for children ages two to four. In the same sense, your work is just for the people the company has chosen to be there.

- Can you think of a time your child might be able to go with you? Can you take him or her into work for a short time in the evening or weekend sometime in the near future? If you can, let them know when they can go with you and mark it on the calendar. That will give them something to look forward to and it also helps establish when it is appropriate for them to come to your workplace and when it is not.

- Explain to your child who else will be there. Point out that they are all adults and that there will be no other children to play with.

- Tell your child what you have to do when you get there. Make sure they know that you won't have any time to spend with them.

Books for Young Children
Working by Jean Claverie
Daddies, What They Do All Day by Helen Walker Puner
Mommies at Work by Eve Merriam
Mommy's Office by Barbara Shook Hazen
My Father's Luncheonette by Melanie Hope Greenberg

WHEN WILL YOU BE COMING HOME?

Both of my children have a fundamental need to know when I will be home. It doesn't usually matter how long I will be gone as long as they know when they can expect to see me again. They need to know if I will be there to tuck them into bed or if I will check on them when I return from a late night meeting. If I say I will be there by bedtime—and I am not—I hear about it the next day. My older son told me that he "stores" things to tell me while I am gone. If I am not there for him to purge it all out at the appointed time, it throws his sense of balance off. They just want to know what to expect.

—Joanna

Children not only need to know when you will be returning from an absence, but they also need some warning as to when you will be leaving. This is especially true if your children are very young and you will be away overnight. Giving them the tools to anticipate your arrivals and departures helps them prepare mentally for your absences. It also gives them a better chance to accept your leaving and to have some control over their own feelings. All of this will translate into easier, stress-free goodbyes and smoother returns for you.

The way you prepare your children for your departure and subsequent arrival all depends upon how well your child understands the concept of time. If they can work abstractly, then you can easily use clocks and calendars to get the message across. If they are very young, then you can use games or visual methods to help them grasp the passage of time.

I remember a time when my daughter was in kindergarten and I left her at the after-school program. I had told her I would return in less than an hour. She called me after about twenty minutes, crying and wondering where I was. She commented that I had been gone for such a long time. I realized then that she had no sense of what an hour was.

—Rose

Children Understanding Time

- The age a youngster is able to understand the concept of time varies from child to child. Pick a method that fits well with your child's developmental level.

- Very young children may understand the concept of time as it relates to the natural segments of their day—breakfast, lunch, nap, dinner and bedtime. All references to time can be made around these time periods.

- If you are trying to explain to a very young child how long you will be gone, pick an increment of time that they will understand. Use "the amount of time you are at the babysitter's (or daycare)" or "how long it takes you to watch _____ " (a favorite television show) as a measuring device for them. If they have a favorite video, use that. "I will be gone just as long as it takes you to watch _____."

- Older children who are learning how to tell time can be shown on the clock when you are leaving and returning. See **The Matching Clocks** on page 26.

- If you will be away on a trip—even for one night—a more detailed approach is needed. See the sections on **Preparing for Your Trip** on page 94 and **Counting the Days Until You Return** on page 103. They describe wonderful ways to graphically show young children how long it will be until you return home.

Books for Young Children
Tick-Tock by Eileen Brown
Clocks and More Clocks by Pat Hutchins
Big Time Bears by Stephen Krensky
When by Leo Leonni
The Tomorrow Book by Doris Schwerin
Watch That Watch by Hila Colman
Clocks and How They Go by Gail Gibbons

A TIME TELLING ACTIVITY

Here's how to use your absences as opportunities for teaching children how to tell time. Try this activity to help them understand both how clocks work and when you are returning home. Young children will have a lot of fun running to see if the two clocks match. Depending on the age of your child, it may also be a good time to purchase their very first wristwatch.

THE MATCHING CLOCKS

1. Draw the appropriate clock face—digital or traditional.
2. Using a colorful marker or crayon, you or the adult at home can draw in the time you will return. Be sure to allow for bad traffic, staying a little longer at work, picking up dinner, or any other thing that might delay your return.
3. Hang up or prop the clock face next to a similar clock in your house.
4. Ask the adult at home to show your child how the running clock changes in order for it to match the clock which you drew.
5. Have the adult at home explain that when the two clocks match, you will be home.

Who Will Take Care of Me?

I would leave for work early so I could hang around in the morning at their daycare for maybe a half hour or so. I intentionally became very good friends with my caregiver. We would do things as families outside of daycare. We always planned a special event at Christmas time for her kids and mine. We would go to breakfast, and then go Christmas shopping. We have done this ritual for five years. As our relationship evolved, our caregiver would keep our children overnight and then I would keep her kids overnight. I am still friends with this person. Getting to know your caregiver and even your children's teachers is critical. If you make the caregiver feel like family, it doesn't feel like your children are going to an outsider's house—to either you or them.

—Mary

If your absence is a routine one, and your child is going to be cared for by their other parent or their usual daycare provider or babysitter, then you won't need to elaborate much on the answer to this question. If, however, you are leaving your child with a new caregiver, then who will care for them can be uppermost in their mind. They need to feel—above all else—that it will be someone they can trust. Older children probably also want to know that it is someone who will be both caring and fun.

For these reasons, it is necessary to paint a picture ahead of time of who will care for them during your absence and what they will do. Anticipating their anxieties can do wonders in easing their worries about your leaving. If they think they will be well cared for and happy, it will be much easier for them to let you go out the door without a struggle.

What Your Children Need to Know About Their Caregiver

- Tell your children who is coming. If it is a new babysitter and your children are young or shy, arrange a meeting for all of them ahead of time. Be sure to mention some things the new caregiver will do with them—play games, take them swimming, or go to the park. If at all possible, arrange some overlap time between the arrival of the new babysitter and your departure so your children can adjust to the new sitter's presence.

- If you will be gone overnight, and the sitter is new, make sure to plan one or two short sitting dates first, so everyone will have a chance to become more comfortable around each other before spending prolonged time together.

- Describe how long the caregiver will be there and tell your children what he or she will do for them—such as getting them up, helping with their bath, or putting them to bed.

- Clue the caregiver in about any special twists on the routine in your home. Try to think of anything the children will expect from them ahead of time to fend off any disappointment that could result from the babysitter not meeting their expectations.

- Sit down with your older children and make a list of all the privileges you allow them because of their age such as watching a special TV show, reading in bed, or playing outside in the yard by themselves. Assure them that you will give this list to the new caregiver.

- Leave an activity that you know will be a successful one for your children. This will do wonders for the new sitter's popularity.

- If your children are switching to a new daycare provider, make sure they are familiar and comfortable with their new routine before you leave town.

Books for Young Children
Uncle Elephant by Arnold Lobel
Come Play With Us by Anne Sibley O'Brien
Going to Daycare by Fred Rogers
Will You Come Back for Me? by Ann Tompert
The New Sitter by Ruth Abel
Don't Forget to Come Back by Robie Harris
The Goodbye Book by Judith Viorst
The Baby-Sitter by Linda Duczman

3
BUILDING THE LINES
OF COMMUNICATION

I would do things like have lunch a couple of times a month at daycare. I would call them if I could at a designated time like right after nap. I would stick a little note in their lunch box for the caregiver to read to my child. I needed to do things like that which would make me feel connected to them.

—Mary

In the last chapter you learned how to give your children a sense of where you are going, why you have to go there, and when you are coming home. Sometimes, even with those questions answered in their minds, they need some reassurance or contact with you while you are gone. It usually takes the form of a phone call, but it can be so much more. We have, at our fingertips, many more ways of conveying our love than picking up the phone. This chapter will help you reach out and touch them from a distance using many of the other techniques available.

TELEPHONE MAGIC

I am a self-employed accountant. For about six months, I was traveling to and working in native Alaskan villages. With small airplanes going in and out of these villages and no jet service, there was many a time I would be weath-ered in—unable to get back to Anchorage. I would pack whatever chapter book we were reading at the time, and I would call my children. They would put me on the speaker phone, and I would read the next chapter or so in the book over the phone. I would then tell my children about the village I was in, where I was sleeping, and what kind of food I was eating. Tasting seal meat and taking steam baths with the Yupik Eskimos made for some interesting bedtime stories.

—Pati

Talking on the telephone with loved ones is the next best thing to being there. Actually hearing the voice of a special person gives us a feeling of connection. The telephone allows us to convey messages, allay fears, whisper words of love, encourage each other, and relate important instructions. The telephone allows us to continue our relationships with each other when we are physically separated, and sometimes a quick phone call can mean the world to a child who misses you. If you are going away on a trip, phone contact can be crucial to helping them feel in touch with you.

The physical setup of the telephone system in your home can further enhance communication between you and your children. Although your basic telephone works just fine, a cordless telephone with a speaker base, automatic dialing and a message machine offers the greatest flexibility.

A cordless phone means that your call can come to any family mem-ber, even when they are busy elsewhere in your home, and it also allows anyone to have conversations in private. If you have a speaker feature on your system, everyone can get into the act for a family conversation, or it can bring your voice and presence into the room for a child either too reluctant or angry to talk with you. Memory or automatic dialing allows you to program in the number where you can be reached so a small child can call you, while a message machine lets you communicate with your family when your call reaches an empty house.

If you have toddlers who may not get any practice using the phone, start them out with phone calls at home on a play phone. Explain that they need to speak their answers, not nod their heads "yes" and "no." When they become comfortable with that, call them at a prearranged time for some "real-life" practice in using your home telephone. That way, if you have to travel, you won't be breaking in a new skill and trying to communicate at the same time.

PHONE ACTIVITIES FOR YOU

- Pick a time and call your children at the appointed hour or have them call you at work. That way, they have a definite contact time to look forward to. Have the adult at home set a timer or alarm clock to go off at that time or use **The Matching Clocks** on page 26. (Hint: Don't do this unless you know you will be available at the designated time.)

- If you are away for more than one day and you are able to call each day, ask your children a riddle or tell them the beginning of a joke one evening, then tell them the answer in the following day's phone call—if they haven't already figured it out.

- If you are on a trip, describe your hotel room, the weather and the day's events when you call. If you have very young children, sometimes the little details, such as the food you eat or a description of a statue in the lobby, are especially meaningful.

- If you call and the family is not at home, leave a message for each member of the family on the message machine. That makes everyone, even older children, feel important. You'll be surprised how often they play back the message.

- Leave a "welcome home from school or daycare" message on your answering machine for your children.

- If you have voice mail, let your children leave one message a day for you on your voice mail.

Children and telephones can often be a natural pairing when it comes to activities. If they are older, they probably have a telephone glued to their ear much of the time anyway. Include your children in the phone activities described on the next page.

Phone Activities for Your Children

- Ask them to practice a song, poem or speech and to recite it to you when you call.

- Tell them they can think up a new recording for your answering machine. Suggest that they practice it and then record the new message. Kids love to do this, and the message can be changed every week or so.

- Ask your child if they will be your secretary while you are away. Give them a telephone message book and ask them to record and organize your telephone messages.

- If you have young children, have the adult at home teach them how to dial the telephone number where you can be reached. It is important, though, to stress that they need to have permission from an adult to call you, or you might have phone calls from them every ten minutes!

- If you will be away on a trip, help your child program your telephone numbers into the telephone. If you program long distance numbers into your phone's automatic dialing feature, you might also want to educate your children about the proper times to make those long distance calls. Young children—in their explorations about your home—can pick up the phone and call the numbers by mistake. Either keep the phone out of young children's reach, or supervise them when they use it. You don't want a long distance phone bill full of calls your two-year-old made!

Books for Young Children
The Telephone by Korney Chukovsky
Telephone Time by Ellen Weiss

Cellular Phones

I use our cell phone with our children right now. They know that they can give me a call if they need anything. Mostly they call to find out if they can have a certain food for snack, or to get permission to do something. Only once has it been anything significant. My daughter got scared because a woman had been sitting in a car out in front of our house for a long time. The only problem was that I had left work to go get my hair highlighted. I had to leave the salon with tin foil wrapped all over my head, go home, pick the kids up, and bring them back with me so that the beautician could finish my highlights! The woman in front of my house turned out to be waiting for her child to get off the school bus! So I looked like a fool for twenty minutes in traffic—big deal.

—Heidi

Cellular phones are wonderful since they provide immediate communication between the family at home and a parent who would otherwise be incommunicado. This can be especially important if one of your children is sick or going through a troubling time. Ask your friends and colleagues where you can get the best deal on a cellular phone. To help your child learn about your cell phone, assist them in filling out the worksheet **Cellular Phone Basics** found on page 183.

The important things to remember about cellular phones are that you must be within your own phone's range for it to work and that you are often charged by the minute for using it. Make sure your children know your rules regarding the use of your cellular phone. Check with your phone plan's customer service representative if you are in doubt about the range of your phone.

My daughter, Kayli, usually just calls me on my cell phone when she is planning sleepovers and trips to the mall. My son, Cory, calls all the time no matter what kind of question he has. The other week he called me and asked me, "Dad, do I really have to eat these lima beans?" His nanny had told him he had to eat them, and he was looking for a way out of it. So there we sat, using this expensive phone time talking about lima beans.

—Doug

CELLULAR PHONE ACTIVITIES FOR ALL OF YOU

- Call your children from the car or a strange place. Describe to them where you are.

- Let them use the cellular phone to call someone from a strange place.

- If you are working on-site or out of the office, set a time for your children to call you on your cellular.

- Take the cellular phone with you and your child on an outing and arrange for someone to call your child.

I'll use the cell phone to call my kids to let them know that my plane has landed and I am on my way to get them. It gives them time to get ready for me—both to pack up their stuff and to shift gears mentally. The cell phone also gives them a way to touch base with me if they feel a need. I've also called them a few times from the phones on the airplane.

—Jan

TAPING LOVE MESSAGES ON A CASSETTE PLAYER

Cassette recorders have been a part of our lives since my older son was about two. We have recorded hilarious toddler descriptions of the mundane events in our lives, taped friends singing and laughing, and we've conducted many a "man-on-the-street interview." Leaving a secret message, then telling the child about it, has produced many a squeal of delight. The tape recorder we have now is one of those indestructible ones made for kids and my four-year-old carries it around the house with him sometimes. Listening now to some of those earlier tapes is fun for all of us.

—Joanna

Children love listening to their own recorded voices. They can while away a lot of time recording silly little messages and songs and playing them back. Why not use this fun device as a mode of communicating while you are away? The goal is to get messages flowing back and forth between you and your children. Start out by making cassette tapes for them. Then either you or the adult at home can help them make a few of their own. Chances are that when you get them started, they will think up tape ideas of their own and be off and running. Who knows, relatives that live far away might benefit from a few tapes sent to them after the kids get the hang of it.

My kids loved to listen to themselves on cassette recorders when they were younger. I used to interview them and they would play it back at night. They loved hearing their own voices answering my questions.
—Heidi

CASSETTE RECORDER BASICS

• Ideally, everyone needs their own personal cassette player. That way, everyone will feel comfortable making their messages personal and/or confidential. Your children can then also play your messages when they want to, not according to their siblings' needs.

• You and your older children may prefer a Walkman type or the handheld version of the cassette recorder.

• Young children like indestructible models made especially for toddlers with big colorful buttons that distinguish PLAY from RECORD.

• Make sure you have lots of blank tapes on hand at any one time. Buy them in bulk at a discount store to save money. Remember, you don't have to buy the best quality tape. Even the cheapest ones record voice quality well enough for these purposes. You also want to buy the shortest ones (sixty minutes or less) because most of the messages are short ones.

• Each time you make a tape, label it before you record it. You don't want to spend a lot of time recording several tapes for your children, and then have to listen to them to find out which one is which.

• When recording on a tape, include the day of the week or the date the message is intended for. If you are going out of town and you want your child to play the message the following Wednesday, mention it on the tape. For example: "It's Wednesday now, and I've been gone for two days. I'm really missing you now!... (insert rest of message) ...."

- Give each child a personal tape of their own and encourage them to record their tapes in privacy if they wish.

- Jot down what you want to say in outline form before you start to record, or wing it and just say whatever pops into your mind.

The kinds of messages you can include on your tapes are virtually unlimited. Start with the following suggestions to get you started, and then for additional ideas, just think about your family's daily routine. Do your children have a long drive to school or daycare? If so, make a tape for them to play while they are in the car. Do they have a hard time getting up in the morning? Would **A Good Morning From Me** tape like the one mentioned below add a little novelty to their day and help roust them out of bed?

TAPES YOU CAN MAKE FOR YOUR CHILDREN

- **(Your Child's Name)'s Good Night Tape:** Use this tape to give each child a special "good night" and to tell them how much you love and miss being a part of their routine. See the section, **Bedtime Bonds from a Distance**, on page 83 for more bedtime activities.

- **A Good Morning from Me:** How do you usually greet your child in the morning? Do you sing a song, whisper in their ear, or call to them? Record what you normally say, or start a new routine by recording a different wake-up call.

- **When I Am Away for the Evening:** If you will only be gone for an evening, record a quick personal message for each child. They will know you thought about them in advance of your absence.

- **When I Am Away on a Trip:** If you will be gone for more than one day, prerecord a different message for each day you will be gone. The messages need not be long ones, and you can generally describe what you think you will be doing each day. Here's an example: "It's Tuesday, Brian, and I'm in Atlanta. I have meetings today, and then I'm going to take an airplane to St. Louis. You have a good time at Jenny's house today. I love you."

- **A Prayer Tape:** This can be meaningful if you and your children pray together and you are going to be away.

- **Favorite Songs:** Make a tape of the songs you and your children share. Get your children in on the act for this one and take turns singing them, or sing them all together. If you play an instrument, tape yourself playing your children's favorite songs.

- **I Love You Because...** or **You Are Special Because...:** Tell your child all the reasons you think they are unique and special.

- **Loving Family and Friends:** Make a tape that lists all the people that love your child.

If you travel, little mementos could accompany each taped message. During the message, the parent could tell the child where a surprise is located. This memento should be small and meaningful to the child. What is special to your child? A drawing pen, a photograph, a bag to put things in, sports cards, a new item for a collection of theirs, a cookie? These are all possibilities. Remember to keep the favors simple and personal.

My older son, who is twelve now, went to Africa with his grandfather and two cousins last Christmas vacation. He went to Egypt and floated down the Nile and to a Masai village in Kenya. I made some cassette tapes for him to listen to along the way.

—Heidi

Making tapes can really be fun when everyone gets in on the act. Your children can make tapes of happenings while you are away, or make a tape for you to play on your trip. If your child is not much of a talker, have someone ask them specific questions.

TAPES YOUR CHILDREN CAN MAKE FOR YOU

- **What Went On In My Day:** This is a running commentary your child makes at night about their day. In the beginning, they, or whoever is helping them, might want

to use the checklist below to help them think about what to say.
- Where did you go today? (school, friend's house, church, riding bikes, lessons)
- What did you do when you got there?
- What was the weather like?
- How did you feel today: happy, sad, mad, excited or a combination?
- What was the best part of the day?
- What was the worst part of the day?
- Did you have any problems today?
- Did anything funny happen today?
- Was there anything special you wanted to talk about with your mom or dad?

- **Our Together Tape:** This tape is reserved for events, activities or plans your child wants to do with you. Any time your child thinks of something he or she wants to do with you, whether you are there or not, they simply pop the tape in and record it. When you get home, or when you have a weekend day free, you can both listen to the list of activities and pick one. The next time your child says, "I want to go see that new movie," instead of feeling guilty about saying, "Not today, I have to work," tell them to go put it on **Our Together Tape** so you will be sure and not forget it when you do have time.

- **Family Silliness:** This is a tape kids love to make. Pass the cassette recorder around and everyone gets to have their turn at being silly. You can sing, yodel, tell a joke—it really doesn't matter. Listening to this tape can be just as fun as making it!

- **The Family News:** The kids act as reporters and make a recorded family newsletter. They can interview each family member, friends and neighbors about happenings around your house or neighborhood.

- **Dear (Mom/Dad):** Ask your child to record a letter to you while you are gone. If you are away for the evening, they can leave it on your pillow. If you are on a trip, they can mail it to you, or make it a running letter that continues each day until you return.

You'll be amazed how these tapes can start to multiply. Save the tapes. Date, label and store them, and you will have a box of preserved memories to take out whenever you want to remember wonderful family times from the past.

WRITING FEELINGS IN JOURNALS

A journal can be a great way for your child to record memories in one place. Journals help young children gather their thoughts. Journals can also be a powerful communication tool between you and your children, and between you and the adult at home caring for your children.

To help make the art of journal writing appealing to your children, give each child their own journal so it will be available to them when they want to use it. Preschoolers and young children need a large format journal—a large tablet is ideal. They also tend to use them up rather quickly, so don't spend a lot of money on a special book. Older children can choose whatever appeals to their personality—a spiral-bound notebook, a diary with a lock and key, or a brightly colored bound blank book. Show them some of these options and let them make a selection. A special pen or pencil can also be purchased.

STARTING THE JOURNAL HABIT

It's not enough to simply place a notebook and a pen in front of a child to start them on a regular routine of using a journal. They need to wet their feet a little bit before plunging into it. Try out some of the activities below to help them get started or when they are stumped for ideas.

 ## ACTIVITIES FOR NEW WRITERS

- **Drawing or painting a picture in the journal:** If your child is young, the adult at home can label parts of it or write a story the picture(s) inspired.

- **A checklist of chores:** If your child is young, he or she can put a sticker on the page as each chore is completed.

- **A wish list:** Toys they want, things they want to do, trips they would like to take

- **A list of books:** Ones they have read, have had read to them, or would like to enjoy in the future

- **Creative writing:** Try a short story or a poem.

- **The day's treasures:** Paste tickets, brochures, leaves, pictures, or a flower onto the pages.

- **Collages:** They can make pictures using colorful cuttings from pages of magazines.

- **Lessons:** They can practice writing their ABCs or 123s.

- **Names:** They can practice writing names—theirs, family members', or a name belonging to a pet, friend or relative.

- **Drawings you suggest:**
  - the family
  - their favorite animal
  - their friends
  - their house

 Books for Young Children
Writing by Richard Allington
Writing It Down by Vicki Cobb
I Write It by Ruth Krauss
I Can Write by Dr. Seuss

STAY-IN-TOUCH JOURNALING FOR YOUR CHILDREN

After they get the hang of it, your children can use their journals as the place where they tell you all the things that crop up in their minds when you are not there. When you come home and ask what happened that day, instead of saying "Nothing," your children can look at their journals and fill you in on the important events in their lives. Here are some ideas of what to include:

Journal Activities for Your Children

- A written log or drawing of their activities while you were gone

- A record of the day's events at school

- A description of a special activity of theirs that you will miss

- A list of things your child wants the two of you to do when you return

- A letter to you while you are away

- Anything they want to tell you or ask you when you return

- If your children can write, check out these books that show how creative children's journals can be:
  - *Amelia's Notebook* by Marissa Moss
  - *Amazon Diary: The Jungle Adventures of Alex Winters* by Hudson Talbott and Mark Greenburg
  - *Penny Pollard's Diary* by Ann James

STAY-IN-TOUCH JOURNALING FOR YOU

A journal can be a wonderful outlet for you as well. You can use it as a gathering place for your thoughts at the end of the day—a place for reflection about all of life's events. Finally, your journal can act as a confidant and trusted friend. If your feelings are particularly strong, your journal gives you a perfect place to vent them. Recording your feelings gives you a chance to look at them later in a calmer light. Your journal can be an exciting tool for your personal growth.

JOURNAL ACTIVITIES FOR YOU

- If you are away from home, keep a journal of your activities and share it with your children when you return.

- When you are away, writing at night in your journal can also help connect you mentally to your family and friends back home.

- Record major events and accomplishments at work. Write out your frustrations from work as well.

- Write about things on your mind. Are you stewing about anything at night? Vent it in your journal.

- Jot down any things your child did that day worth remembering. Sometimes waiting even one day can make the difference between remembering and forgetting a precious moment.

- Write about the joys and the tears of parenting and partnering.

I've kept a journal since my daughter was born. I don't write in it every day—or even every week sometimes. I write in it to tell her about what life is like growing up with her in these crazy times. I write about what she is doing, what she likes and dislikes, and what is going on in the world. I write it like a letter to her—something she might read when she is in college. It all started when I asked my mother about something soon after my own daughter was born. She said she truly did not remember. I decided I wanted to try and capture as much of this time as I could.

—Rose

STAY-IN-TOUCH JOURNALING FOR THE ADULT AT HOME

Journals can also be used as a means of communication between you and your partner or caregiver at home. They can work especially well in keeping a traveling parent in touch. If the adult at home doesn't enjoy writing, ask them to jot down a word or two that will trigger their memory upon your return. So many things can happen in the lives of young children in a short period of time. They learn, they grow, they experience new things every moment. They say and do funny and endearing things all the time. A journal gives your partner or caregiver an ideal place to record some of those things that you miss. Show them the list below to give them ideas of what you would be interested in hearing upon your return.

My son's teacher kept a journal when he was in an intensive preschool program. It was a great tool not only for communication purposes, but also to measure progress and growth. I saved these—three and one-half years' worth—and perhaps someday he can read them and learn a little about himself.
—Mary

JOURNAL ACTIVITIES FOR THE ADULT AT HOME

- List funny or special things the children did or said.

- Chronicle any developmental milestones reached by the children.

- Write about any difficulties the children encountered.

- Make notes of any changes in the children's normal behavior.

- Record school or daycare news, schedule changes, sports/activity information.

- List any questions that arose that only the absent adult can answer.

- Keep track of phone messages.

- Insert news clippings of interest.

- Jot down problems that need discussion.

- Make a note of upcoming plans or events.

I wish I had kept a journal in a notebook when my children were young. I used to write pages to their caregiver about what was on the schedule each day and what tricks each was trying to pull that week. One time my mom watched my children for me and I had two pages—front and back—written about their behavior. She looked at me and said, "When will I ever have the time to read this?" When I got home though, she said, "They did everything you mentioned on those sheets of paper!" I wish I had those now.

—Heidi

STAY-IN-TOUCH JOURNALING FOR THE FAMILY

After your children have had a chance to familiarize themselves with writing in a journal, you can try communicating with them through journal writing the next time you are away. There are many ways to establish a back and forth conversation between you and your children through journals. You can alternate with your child writing in their journal, or you can start a family journal expressly for this purpose.

Ask your children if it is all right for you to write in their journal, or if they want to keep it private. If privacy is an issue, get a new book that is fair game for every member of your family. Any one can write in it any time they like. If everyone gets involved, it can be as exciting for young children as getting mail. Get them started by writing something and then casually drop the question, "I wonder if anyone has checked the family journal recently?" Be sure to tell your children that the journal is a place to preserve all kinds of things—funny incidents, jokes, pictures and photos to name a few.

FAMILY JOURNAL ACTIVITIES

- Write a personal message in the family journal for each member of your family.

- If you will miss bedtime, write a personal "good night" in the family or children's journals.

- Write a question for everyone in the family to answer in the journal. You will end up with some fun written "snapshots" of the whole family. Sample questions:
  - What is your favorite color/animal/friend/sport/activity?
  - What do you want to be when you grow up and why?
  - What do you like best about school/work?
  - What do you like least about school/work?
  - What would you do tomorrow if you could do anything?

- If you are having a family problem, you can use the journal to start a dialog about each family member's viewpoint. Journals give you a neutral place to "talk" and problem solve.

- Write an opening line to a story and have each member of your family add five or six sentences. Continue the story until it sounds done. Have a family reading one night. Sample Openers:
  - Once upon a time...
  - The day I stumbled upon the castle was just the beginning...
  - It was a dark and scary night when...
  - One day I opened the door to our home, and I saw...

Books for Young Children
Guess Who My Favorite Person Is? by Byrd Baylor

FINAL THOUGHTS ON JOURNALING

Try getting the journaling routine started when you are home. If you can't find the time in your regular routine, try creating journal events where you all sit down and work in your journals together. If you keep a journal, share with your children moments you have written about—their birth, a milestone in their life, or the events of a trip you have recorded. When they see how you have captured those precious moments, they are much more likely to want to capture a few of their own.

SENDING LOVE MESSAGES THROUGH THE MAIL

One thing we do that the kids really like is to go to a copy center and get the kids' artwork put on postcards. They copy it onto card stock which is heavy enough to mail as a postcard. Then my husband takes the postcards on his trip and sends them home to the kids. They get a kick out of seeing their artwork come through the mail.

—Jeannie

Everyone adores receiving mail from someone they love. Children are no different. Postcards sent from your workplace reassure a child that you have been thinking about them while at work. Receiving postcards with pictures of your hotel and scenes from the places you visit can also be very exciting for a child. Even if the postcards don't arrive until after you have returned, your children will have a feeling of being included in your time away from home. The postcards may even be the start of a new hobby—stamp or postcard collecting.

POSTCARD AND LETTER ACTIVITIES FOR YOU

- Collect regional postcards and hotel stationery and give or send them to your children. You can also save them and send them a postcard or letter from work every so often. You don't have to be out of town.

- Sit down and talk about the pictures shown on postcards you have collected—describe your impressions of the places they picture.

- Paste a postcard on the back of a family photograph and turn the photo into a postcard. Mail it to your children and let them wonder how a photograph of them became a postcard.

- Write a postcard or letter to be tucked into their lunch box or daycare bag.

- Mail a postcard or letter from the airport as you leave town on a trip. Or send one a day or two before you leave. That ensures that your children will get mail soon after your departure.

- Send numbered postcards or letters with messages that either build on each other or are written a few words at a time per postcard. This works well if you are going to be gone for a week or more.

- If your trip is a short one, write the postcards or letters ahead of time and have the adult at home give them to your children each day. Or have the adult at home plant them in the mail box for your children to receive with the daily mail. You can paste a stamp on it to make it look more authentic.

- Don't forget about overnight delivery services such as Federal Express, United Parcel Service or the Post Office. If you have something important to send to your child, or if you simply want them to feel very important and special, send them an overnight letter with a little treat tucked inside. It will make their day!

I was helping out at school and I saw a girl pull out a napkin from her lunchbox with a note on it from one of her parents. A gesture that small can really make a difference.

—*Heidi*

Children love to make and send postcards almost as much as they love receiving them. If they have a ready supply at home, they can launch into a game of post office, or mail delivery, or begin designing postcards at any time. Some of the following activities help them learn about the whys and wherefores of mail delivery as well.

POSTCARD AND LETTER ACTIVITIES FOR YOUR CHILDREN

- Take your children to the store and let them pick up a supply of postcards or stationery to have on hand or have the adult at home take them to the store during your trip. They can pick out a postcard to surprise you.

- Let your children use their postcard or stationery supply to write on, play post office, or to actually send a note.

- Purchase blank postcards or cut out a postcard size piece of cardboard and let them design their own. If you have time, have the adult at home help them mail it to you, a friend or a relative.

- Let your children draw a postcard or letter instead of writing it. If your child is young, have the adult at home ask them to describe the picture and label it for you.

- If you are on a trip, have the children make up funny addresses to put on the postcards and have them keep the cards at the house for your return instead of mailing them.

- Organize a field trip to the post office. Call ahead to find out how to arrange a behind-the-scenes tour for your children and the adult who supervises them when you are gone.

- Match your older children up with a pen pal. Use the following addresses or the websites on page 190 to get matched up with a pen pal in a different country:

World Pen Pals
1690 Como Avenue
Dept. BL
St. Paul, Minnesota 55108
Enclose a self-addressed, stamped business envelope for their latest set of instructions.

Friends Forever Pen Pal Club
P.O. Box 753
Planetarium Station
New York, NY 10024-0753
Send a self-addressed, stamped envelope for their latest requirements. These pen pals are primarily ages seven and up.

Books for Young Children
The Jolly Postman by Janet and Allen Ahlberg
Stringbean's Trip to the Shining Sea by Vera Williams
Mr. Grimes by Cynthia Rylant
Dear Daddy by Philippe Dupasquier
Messages in the Mailbox by Loreen Leedy
Don't Forget to Write by Martina Selway
Dear Annie by Judith Caseley

TYPING TENDER MESSAGES ON YOUR COMPUTER

My husband's younger daughter lives in Colombia with her mother. He e-mails her all the time. We also use e-mail a lot when there are details to be worked out about her coming to visit.

—Jan

A computer performs a lot of functions for a family; it educates, organizes and provides entertainment. It also offers each member of the family a unique opportunity to get in touch with people all over the world through the Internet. There are many ways to use your computer to communicate with your children while you are gone. E-mail, word-processing software and some educational software are ideal for this purpose. Be sure to check out the software and websites listed in **Appendix C: Resources by Chapter** on page 187.

You can get film developed on a disk which allows you to load the images into your computer. You could then do all kinds of things—use some of the images as your screen saver, or send them to the parent at work as an attachment to e-mail. If you are traveling, you could have photos you have taken on your trip put on disk and send them to your family with your e-mail as well.

—Richard

COMPUTER ACTIVITIES FOR YOU

- On-line Activities:
  - Send your children an e-mail message they can read when they get home for the day.
  - Surf the Internet with your children and look for weather information or explore the home pages of the cities you will be visiting when you travel.
  - If you are traveling, send your children an e-mail message each day with some information about where you are and what you are doing. Ask them a question and have them e-mail back their response.

- Activities Without Going On-line:
  - Create a personal screen saver message on your computer to surprise your children.

- If you have a child who knows his way around your computer system, create a file with a small message in it, then hide it in a directory. Give your child some clues—or the file name itself— then let them search for it.
- Make up a certificate of congratulations on your word-processing or publishing software for your children to commemorate any accomplishment.
- Create a word-processing file with a name everyone is familiar with. Have this be an electronic family journal which everyone can use to send messages to each other.

Don't leave your children out where the computer is concerned. They will get a kick out of creating stories, books and drawings on the computer to show to you when you return. If your children are independent computer users, give them a few suggestions and turn them loose at the keyboard. Many children will need help from the adult at home for most of these activities, so make sure the adult or caregiver has the time to lend a hand. If you have a modem, you may want to establish some ground rules for surfing the Internet before you suggest any of these activities.

My daughter and I e-mail back and forth frequently. She is only in the second grade and her sentence structure doesn't come out like she wants it to, but I'm sure it will get easier for her as she gets older.
—Candi

 ## Computer Activities for Your Children

- If you have an e-mail account, suggest your children send you e-mails when they want to get in touch with you.

- Install an easy-to-use word-processing program so your children can write letters to you.

- Some programs allow your children to create books. The younger ones can make pages full of illustrations, while the older ones can add a story line to their pictures. It's a wonderful way for them to illustrate what happened while you were gone, and it's also another way to add pictures to their journal.

- When you are away on a business trip, ask the adult at home to help your children search the Internet for information about where you are. Make sure the adult at home understands who needs to be supervised while on-line.

- Many programs allow both you and your children to make stationery, greeting cards and postcards to send to each other. Have your children design and print out their own personal stationery.

- If one of your children spends a lot of time playing computer games, have them keep track of their new high scores to share them with you when you get home.

Books for Young Children
The Brave Little Computer by David Lyon
The Little Red Computer by Ralph Steadman
Skeeter and the Computer by Frank Modell

My kids e-mail back and forth with my husband. They had an e-mail address at school. They would e-mail messages back to him and get quite a dialog going. We have saved some of their e-mails with more creative spelling. My daughter sent the e-mail below to Kit in the third grade:
—Heidi

Subject: Impotance
Dad,
Mom told me to emil you tell you that we need to get a Hotel for vacation in May. Besides I raelly do not want to sleep woth the fire ants!!! Oh dad I fowned some good advice on the internet last night. It was tittled as "tips for good hotels" I think? And dad, if you find some things email me back and I will respond!!!
I LOVE YOU
Emma

FRIENDLY FAXES

It's worked great the times we have faxed back and forth. When my husband travels, he lets us know what the fax number at the hotel is. I was in Palm Springs last year and my husband and the kids sent me a three page fax. It was wonderful. He typed first, then my two older girls typed a short note, then my four-year-old dictated something to be typed.

—Jeannie

Most businesses and more and more homes are installing fax machines. Many computers have the capability to send faxes too. The advantage of a fax machine is that it offers immediate visual communication. If there is a picture, document or message which you want your children to see right away, a fax machine is the perfect way to get it to them.

If you don't have the ability to fax from your home and you want to fax something to your family, there are options. When you are at the office or traveling, you can send a fax to a neighbor's machine, your spouse's fax at work, or an independent mail store or copy center near your home. Don't use someone's fax at work, though, without first finding out ahead of time if personal faxes are against office policy. If you are using the fax machine at your hotel, watch out! Those fax charges can build up. Be sure to ask about fax charges before you go wild sending messages to your children from your hotel room.

FAXING ACTIVITIES FOR YOU

• Send a daily greeting to your children—a good morning or welcome home from school or daycare. If you do it regularly, they will start running over to the computer or fax as soon as they get home.

• Send a fax postcard. Copy both sides of a postcard onto a piece of paper, then write in the message just like on a regular postcard.

• Send your family any changes in your schedule or itinerary when you travel.

• Fax your children a drawing you did just for them. Children don't often get to see their parent's drawing efforts and they love it.

- When you travel, if you have liberal use of fax machines, ask your children a question or riddle, then fax them the answer along with a new question the next day.

If you have a machine at home, let your children get into the act. It's a great way for them to learn how a fax machine looks, acts and works.

FAXING ACTIVITIES FOR YOUR CHILDREN

- Ask the adult at home to teach your children how a fax machine works.

- Let your children fax you a homework assignment they have been working on. You can correct it or write something encouraging like *Terrific!* or *Outstanding!* before you fax it back.

- Ask your children to send you a drawing during the day. Give them a specific drawing assignment—like Our Family, My Favorite Holiday, or What I Like To Do Best—if they have trouble thinking of ideas.

- Ask your children to fax you a record of what happened during their day.

MAKING COMMUNICATION EASIER USING *COMMUNICATION CENTRAL*

If you go into my home office, you'll see that I have a Communication Central. I went to the store and got a board and different colored markers for each person in the family. It's been a wonderful thing to have. I feel like I am a very organized person, and it really ties things together for me. Now the kids know where to put any important papers. Before, they were put on the counter in the kitchen, then they got moved, and it was hard to keep track of them.

—Jeannie

There are many ways to communicate, but you can be sabotaged before you start if your house is stuck in information overload. Do you have papers piled up, phone numbers that have somehow disappeared and messages that end up lost in the shuffle? If organization is your problem, **Communication Central** can be the answer to your dilemma. If you find yourself spending precious time at home searching for papers, permissions slips, and school or daycare notices, taking the time to set up a central communication area in your house can give you more free time at home with your children in the long run.

One purpose of **Communication Central** is to provide you and your family with one place for communicating. If you have to be away for an evening, your family can leave you a message to read upon your return. If you forget to tell your children something, you can write a reminder they will see immediately upon coming home from daycare or school.

In addition, frequently used phone numbers, permission slips, schedules and special event notices can be posted and easily accessed time and time again. If you travel, your itinerary can be posted there so no one has to search for it when your family wants to call you.

Don't be intimidated by thinking there is a lot of work involved in setting up **Communication Central**. Once the materials are purchased, it will probably only take you an hour to put it together from start to finish. And that investment of an hour of your time will save you countless hours of searching for numbers, permission slips and notes from your family later.

FIVE REASONS YOUR FAMILY COULD USE COMMUNICATION CENTRAL

- It will give you one central place to post messages to and from family members.

- All your family's important information will be accessible in a moment's notice: daycare notices, school papers, permission slips and phone numbers.

- You will be supremely organized.

- Your caregiver will have all the information he or she needs at their fingertips.

- If you travel, you can easily turn it into a **Ground Control Center** where your family can gather at night to track your trip and feel more in touch with you. (See **Using Ground Control Center to Stay Connected,** page 90.)

SETTING UP *COMMUNICATION CENTRAL*

The first step in making **Communication Central** is to figure out the best place to put it. It should be in a central area of your home where your family will see the information on a daily basis. A bulletin board on a wall or a refrigerator—if it's not covered with photos and artwork already!—will do just fine. It helps if it is near a telephone, but that's not essential.

Start out by gathering the following supplies. Your choice of the first item depends upon where you've decided to locate **Communication Central**. If you are going to use your refrigerator, you will need to get lots of strong magnets (the ones with clips attached are ideal), but if you are mounting it on a wall, then a bulletin board or dry erase board seem to work best.

MATERIALS FOR *COMMUNICATION CENTRAL*

- Bulletin board, dry erase board or magnets for your refrigerator

- A colorful 9" X 12" clasp envelope for each child

- Calendar

- Bin or basket for all your supplies

- Paper and/or Post-it notes

- Pens, pencils, markers and/or erasers

- A copy of the forms in **Appendix A: *Communication Central* Forms** on pages 176-184

BUILDING *COMMUNICATION CENTRAL*

When you have your materials together, use the checklist below to get your ***Communication Central*** up and rolling.

- Mount the bulletin board, the dry erase board, or put the magnets on the front or side of your refrigerator.

- Post the calendar. This will be used to keep track of your family's scheduled activities—not the parent's individual work appointments. When you are making plans, a quick glance will tell you what conflicts exist, if any. Your older children can use it to keep track of your comings and goings from home. If you have a large family or particularly hectic schedules, try using a large format calendar or more than one.

- Label each colored envelope with a child's name, or have each child decorate their own envelope. Hang each envelope by the flap so that it forms a pocket or pouch. Have your children get into the habit of depositing all their important papers—permissions slips, notices, artwork and/or completed school assignments—in their pouch when they return home each day. When you get home, you can sort through the contents of each envelope. Permission slips or papers that need to go back with them are filled out and placed in the pouch for them to retrieve the next morning. Artwork, school work and other papers can be saved, stored or thrown away as you desire.

- Set aside an area designated for messages to and from each other. Put a supply of paper, post-it notes, colorful pens, markers or refrigerator magnets into the supply basket. Use the message area for instructions, reminders to members of your family, and a vehicle for sending messages of love.

- Fill out and post the following forms located on pages 176-184:
  - **Where I Can Be Reached at Work** or **Where I Can Usually Be Reached** for every adult in the family
  - **My Activities and Friends** for each child in the family
  - **Authorization for Medical Care** forms for each child in the family—just in case
  - **Emergency Contact Numbers**
  - **Cellular Phone Basics** and **Pager Basics** (if your family has either of these)

- If you have young children, use pictures of the family to label their envelopes and your schedules. That will give them more of a sense of knowing what is on the board.

- Get started by leaving your family their first message!

COMMUNICATION CENTRAL Ideas

Try a few of the activities below—as well as any in the other sections of this chapter—to christen *Communication Central.*

MESSAGES FOR THE FAMILY

- Leave a **Looking Forward to Seeing You Tonight!** message for each child.

- Post countdown messages for special family events such as **"Three more days until the Fair!"**

- Leave an after-school or after-daycare note telling your children where a special treat can be found.

- Write out a joke or riddle with the punch line either on the back of the paper or in a different spot.

- Write **Congratulations!** or **Job Well Done!** messages for any of your child's accomplishments—even small ones. Leave them up for a few days.

- Let each member of the family have a week to display their favorite art masterpieces.

- Have a **Child of the Week**. Give each child a designated week. Post the child's picture in *Communication Central* and list an accomplishment of theirs every day. One day, have each member of the family write the characteristic they like most about that child.

4
CHASING AWAY BOREDOM AND THE BLUES

My husband used to travel a lot for business. Our son missed him terribly. Sometimes it was simply not enough to tell him when his dad was returning. He needed diversions, he needed consolation, and he needed to know that his dad was thinking about him and had not forgotten him.

—Joanna

What do you do when you miss your family and friends? Do you talk with them on the telephone or plan a special date when they get home? After you have made contact with them, do you seek diversions like calling other people or tackling special projects you have put aside? Your child reacts to your absence in these same ways with one big difference. While you are very capable of reaching out and making sure your needs are met, your children need someone to help them meet theirs.

This chapter offers activities that can be planned by you or given to the adult at home to pull out of the hat whenever the need arises. Use **What to Do When the Kids Are Bored** on page 60 when the situation calls for distractions or entertainment, and sample some of the activities in **What to Do When the Kids Have the Blues** on page 66 for the times when your children really miss you.

A great outside game we have used is to go for a mystery walk. At the corner of the block, you flip a coin, and you walk in the direction the head points. When you can't walk any further in the direction you are going, or when you want a change of pace, flip the coin and go in that direction. We always miraculously end up at the neighborhood store for a treat!

—Mary

—

WHAT TO DO
WHEN THE KIDS ARE BORED

These activities are intended for use by the adult at home when your absence is especially evident. You can pick out the activities for them to try ahead of time, or leave it up to whoever will be with your children. One activity could even be for the adult at home to read all the activities and have the children pick out what sounds the most fun to them.

BOREDOM BUSTER ACTIVITIES

- ### PICK A RESTAURANT
  - Have the children select a favorite restaurant or two that they only visit when you are away. When they get bored, the adult at home can schedule a visit to the restaurant for a pick-me-up.

- ### FOLLOW THE LEADER
  - Play Follow the Leader around the house or apartment. If they want, your children and the adult at home can take a walk around the block or neighborhood and play this game. Everyone should have a chance to be the leader.
  - A variation on Follow the Leader is to give different ways of moving by using a number—for example, 1 is walking, 2 is skipping, 3 is hopping, 4 is walking backwards, and so on. Let the leader call a number, then everyone has to move that way.

- ### CIRCUS NIGHT
  - The children and the adult at home can set the scene by drawing

and cutting out tickets, making popcorn, and building a circus ring by using chairs placed on their side or pillows.
- The children can invite neighbors or friends over and take turns performing their circus "acts." Some ideas for circus acts are:
  —**Lion tamer or trained animal act:** Use the family cat or dog or a stuffed animal.
  —**Acrobat:** The children can turn somersaults, do handstands and headstands, or just jump up and down.
  —**Tight-rope walker:** The child can use an umbrella and "walk" on a rope or string put on the floor.
  —**Strong man:** The child can try to lift several stuffed animals at once.
- If it's nice outdoors, they can have the circus in the yard or a park and use the swings and jungle gym for their acts—especially the trapeze act.

- ## HAVE A PARADE
  - Someone can pick a theme and the adult at home and the children can have a parade around the house or neighborhood.
  - Use a holiday as an excuse for the parade or the adult at home can ask your children to think up a holiday of their own. (See **Family Holiday** activity on the next page.)

- ## FLASHLIGHT TREASURE HUNT
  - The adult at home can instruct the children to go into a different room or sit down and hide their eyes. She can then hide an object that the children are familiar with somewhere in the room.
  - She then turns off the lights and each child tries to find the object while using a flashlight as their source of light.
  - If they have a hard time finding it, she can help them out with clues.

- ## OLYMPICS NIGHT
  - The adult at home can set up different "Olympic events" in your home for your children and maybe some of their friends. She can set up one event for each room or do it all in the biggest room of your house.
  - The children make ribbons or medals to use as prizes for each event.
  - The adult at home acts as announcer and commentator if she is so inspired. Each participant can receive a medal or prize.
  - Some of the events could be as follows:

—hopping on one foot from one side of the room to another
—having a sack race using pillow cases
—having a three-legged race (Two children walk side-by-side with their adjoining legs loosely and safely tied together to form one center leg.)
—carrying a hard-boiled egg or ball on a spoon from one side to another
—constructing an obstacle course out of tables, chairs, pillows and cushions
—trying to go under a limbo stick

- ### FAMILY HOLIDAY
  - The adult at home can talk it over with the children and make up a family holiday. For example, declare a "Family Purple Day" where everyone wears purple, colors purple pictures, drinks grape juice or purple milk, and lists purple things.
  - The possibilities are endless. The evening before is the best time to plan the activities for the holiday celebration and get ready for the event. Activities might include: getting clothes out, making posters, and decorating. You or your caregiver might look in **Advance Activities for Birthdays or Any Holiday** on page 141 for more ideas.
  - Some holiday ideas are:
    —100 Days into the School Year
    —Backwards Day
    —Be Your Favorite Animal Day
    —Queen or King for a Day (where one child gets to be the boss all day)

- ### START A STORY
  - The adult at home starts the story with one or two sentences. Each child adds to the story by adding a sentence or two. Take turns until the story comes to a natural end or the children lose interest.
  - You can write the story down or tape it as you go. The children can illustrate it later. Ask them to save it for you to hear.

- ### PHOTOGRAPH COLLAGES
  - Keep an ongoing box of unused photos that your children can play with.
  - The adult at home can let your child select an assortment of photos from the "discard" box.
  - Your child can then cut and paste them onto the paper any way they want to. They can write funny captions for the pictures or

describe the collage. There could be some interesting information about how they feel about members of the family in their descriptions.
- This activity is good for all ages of children. Older kids can make works of art from old photos.

- PERSONAL PHOTO ALBUMS
  - Have your child pick out a number of his or her favorite family photographs. Either you or another adult can help your child place them into an album.
  - The child then looks at each photo and decides on an appropriate caption.
  - They can then cut out a caption bubble or a rectangle out of paper and someone can write in the caption and place it under the photo.
  - When you get new pictures back, add one or two new photos with captions to their album.
  - Your child can decide on new captions for each photo already in the album as a variation to this activity.

- HOUSEHOLD SCAVENGER HUNT
  - The adult at home can conduct a scavenger hunt with simple objects from around the house.
  - She can call out or make a list of simple household objects and then sit back and watch the kids run around the house and get each one.
  - The hunt can have an alphabet theme. Some examples are:

A - apple, atlas, album	N - newspaper, nail, nut
B - ball, book, basket	O - orange, object, onion
C - crayon, cup, candle	P - pen, pillow, pepper
D - dish, doll, decoration	Q - quilt, quarter, queen card
E - envelope, earring, egg	R - ruler, rubber band, radio
F - fork, food, fan	S - spoon, salt, stuffed animal
G - glass, glove, game	T - towel, teddy bear, train
H - hat, handkerchief, hammer	U - umbrella, unicorn, underwear
I - ice, instrument, insect	V - vacuum, vase, vest
J - jar, jelly, juice	W - watch, wastebasket, wallet
K - key, ketchup, kite	X - Xerox copy, letter X, Xmas item
L - lamp, legos, letter	Y - yarn, yellow, yo-yo
M - magazine, magnet, mop	Z - zipper, zero, zoo animal

- SILLY SUPPOSITIONS
  - One family member comes up with a silly supposition like "What

would you do if a hippopotamus walked in the door right now?" The rest of the family takes turns telling what they would do.

- An absent parent can even be included in it by having the adult at home ask questions like: "What would Mom do if she opened up her briefcase and there were only marshmallows in it?"
- *Mrs. Armitage on Wheels* by Quentin Blake is a good book to set the stage for this game.
- Some silly suppositions to get your children started are:
  —What would you do if you suddenly turned green?
  —What would you do if your house disappeared?
  —What would you do if all your toys were suddenly as big as you?
  —What would you do if you woke up in the morning and we were on Mars?

- ## SECRET CODED MESSAGES

  Using the secret code alphabet below, write a cryptic message on the message area of **Communication Central**, a postcard, a piece of paper or in your family or child's journal. Leave them the secret code to decipher your message—then ask them to send one back to you. Here's how it works:

A	B	C	D	E	F	G	H	I	J	K	L	M
;	o	&	]	|	-	^	$	%	*	"	<	~

N	O	P	Q	R	S	T	U	V	W	X	Y	Z
@	+	\	=	)	(	>	/	x	{	[	:	}

  Example of a cryptic message:

  %   < + x | : + / !

  which, when decoded, means:

  I   L O V E   Y O U !

- ## MAKE-A-MYSTERY
  - **Object of the Game:** Your children will guess a mystery object by using clues you have provided for them.
  - **How to Play**
    1. Pick an object in the house to be the mystery object. For young

children, pick something easy like the refrigerator or a clock. Challenge older children with a specific book, a kitchen utensil or an item of their clothing.

2. If you are away on a trip, your child gets one clue each night. If you are gone for the day, hand out one clue as you leave in the morning and then have the adult at home hand out others at intervals during the day.

3. After receiving each clue, your child gets three guesses before getting the next clue.

4. After guessing the mystery object, the child gets a small treat or prize.

- **A Word About Clues**
  —Start out with general clues at the beginning of the game and get more specific as you go.
  —Use different methods of communication to give your clues: Pass on one clue by telephone, the next clue can come over e-mail, fax, cassette tape or a postcard.
  —If the sample mysteries below are too easy for your children, try giving beginning clues with measurements like "it is 12 inches long" for one clue and "it is 8 inches wide" for the next clue. Be sure your children have access to a ruler if you give measuring clues. Imagine the fun they'll have running around the house measuring everything!

SAMPLE MYSTERY 1

Mystery Object: a clock
Clue 1: It is round.
Clue 2: It is black and white.
Clue 3: It is in the kitchen.
Clue 4: It has writing on it.
Clue 5: The writing is numbers.
Clue 6: It tells us time.

SAMPLE MYSTERY 2

Mystery Object: a blue coat
Clue 1: It is blue.
Clue 2: It is made out of material.
Clue 3: It has pockets.
Clue 4: It has sleeves.
Clue 5: It is in a closet.
Clue 6: It belongs to you.

The busier the kids are, the better they deal with their dad's absence. We just had company during his last trip, and the kids were so busy, they didn't really have time to get blue.

—Jeannie

WHAT TO DO
WHEN THE KIDS HAVE THE BLUES

My older son, Zack, used to have bad dreams. They were really prevalent when Kevin, his dad, was away. When I went to Arizona, I got him a dream catcher with an arrowhead woven into the middle. When I gave it to him, we talked about the dream catcher "catching" all the bad dreams and the sun releasing them to the outside. I can't remember him having many bad dreams since we hung that up.

—Mary

In spite of all the well-meaning activities you may set up for your children, they will still miss your presence. How they manifest this and how they handle it will vary from child to child. One child may beg you to return home at once only to drop the phone midsentence because something else has caught his attention. Another child may genuinely have a case of the blues coloring his mood until you return. Don't use any single absence as a predictor of future problems to come though. Children can go in and out of phases as often as the moon. A child who normally sails through your absences with hardly a notice could be the one moping the next time, while the one who is inconsolable now may be the happy camper next week.

While there is no magic pill you can give your child to ward off the blues, there are coping strategies you can introduce which will help them help themselves. Instead of letting it make you feel guilty every time you have to leave, see it as an opportunity to teach your children coping techniques that can last their lifetime. If business travel is a way of life for your family, you may want to incorporate some of these activities as a part of your pre-trip routine mentioned in **Off on a Trip** on page 89.

BUCKING THE BLUES ACTIVITIES

- **LUCKY CHARM**
  Select something of yours to give your child each time you leave. Explain that the purpose of this "charm" is to help them focus on fun, happy things. Then help your

child make a list of five or ten positive things in their life. When they are feeling sad, they can take out the charm, look at it, and recall the items on their list. With older children, you can talk about them having a choice about how deep and how long they let themselves sink into the blues.

- BLUES TRIGGERS

  Ask your child or the adult at home to use the child's journal to mark down the day, time and what the child was doing when the loneliness set in. Look through the journal upon your return and watch for a pattern. If you can identify triggers for your child's loneliness, you can help prepare for it ahead of time. If you discover patterns, help your child develop a plan of attack for the next time it happens. Make a list of each trigger and think up thoughts or activities that will help your child when that trigger occurs. Be sure to give this list to the adult at home when you leave.

- MISSING YOU

  Schedule a quiet time to sit down with your child and talk about missing people you love. Tell your child that it is very normal to have these feelings and describe some of the times when you've missed them. (Don't overdo it or you might make the child feel responsible for your sadness.) Tell your child some of the things you did to help yourself feel better when you missed them—photos of them, a phone call, getting busy with work, planning an activity for when you next saw them. In addition, help your child choose a few activities that might help. Make a list of these activities to leave with the adult at home. Alert the adult at home of the need to engage in these activities if they notice your child is feeling blue.

- CAPTAIN OF THEIR EMOTIONS

  When your child is in the bathtub, float a toy boat in the water and watch it bob. Point out to your child that there is no captain of the boat, so it just bobs in the water, going nowhere. Then have your child become the captain of the boat by moving the boat back and forth in the water. Explain that as the captain, he or she chooses where the boat goes and how fast it gets there. Now tell your child that he or she is the captain of their feelings too. When they feel sad, they can set the course of their own boat by thinking of happier things to do. Help your child make a list of things to do when they start to feel lonely. Remind them that they are the captain of their ship, and they can start learning right now how to set their emotional course.

- ## THE HAPPY FACE
  Right before you leave, draw a smiling face on their leg or their arm. Tell them this represents your face and it will go everywhere with them while you are apart. They can look at it whenever they wish and think of you drawing it. Be sure to use a permanent type marker that won't come off in the tub if you are going for overnight. If it's okay with you, let them draw a face in an inconspicuous place on you. When you talk on the phone, tell them you look at it every day and think of them.

- ## JUST A PHONE CALL AWAY
  Communicate with your children more often when they are missing you acutely. Call them several times a day if you can. If you will be traveling, make sure to touch base with them each night. This will help you seem more accessible to them. Sometimes a phone call will trigger a crying jag after you hang up. Ask the adult at home to evaluate the effect of your phone calls. If they continue to upset your child, try different forms of communication (see **Building the Lines of Communication** which starts on page 29 for ideas) until you hit on one that helps your child respond positively.

- ## A PET FOR A PAL
  If you travel a lot and your children like animals, consider getting a special pet for your children that will always be there with them. It needn't be a high maintenance pet like a dog or cat. Gerbils, mice, fish and some small birds can be maintained with just a little help by young children. Pick out the pet and help your child gather the things needed to care for the pet. Then when your child gets the blues, he or she can play with the pet and think of the fun you both had making its home.

My older child can become moody when I am gone. I call her just before bedtime when I am out of town, and frequently she is crying. I will ask her to read to me over the phone, and many times that is all it takes to get her out of her sad mood.

—Candi

Bucking the Blues Activities for Your Children and the Adult at Home

• If you travel, the adult at home can help the children remember the success of past trips using photos and mementos. She can get out photo albums or mementos from past trips that will help remind the children that they made it successfully through the trips before.

• The adult at home can suggest that the child write in their journal, draw a picture, or make a collage that expresses their feelings.

• The adult at home can help them plan a surprise to spring when you return.

• The adult at home can suggest the child make one of the cassette tapes mentioned on page 37 for you.

• She can suggest that the child make a welcome home card or poster for you that can be displayed prominently for you to see when you get home.

• She can help the child make a paper doll of you—or of each person in the family. They can gather family photographs that depict family members from head to toe and cut out the body of each family member. They can trace the shape of the body of each family member onto a piece of cardboard and cut it out. Finally, they can glue the photograph onto the cardboard. Some young children will want to carry around or sleep with their paper doll as a way of feeling closer to you.

Books for Young Children

Go Away, Bad Dreams! by Susan Hill

The Little Engine That Could by Watty Piper

You Go Away by Dorothy Corey

When Daddy Comes Home by Linda Wagner Tyler

The Runaway Bunny by Margaret Wise Brown

Waiting for Mom by Lynda Wagner Tyler

Thunder Cake by Patricia Pelacco

If Your Child Is Still Blue. . .

There may be some situations where your child remains despondent about your absences in spite of extra activities and coping strategies. It's time to evaluate the situation from their perspective. How much time have you been able to spend with your children lately? Have you had deadlines or business trips that have taken you away from home more than usual? Could your child simply need a dose of you, or the reassurance that the family routine will revert to normal at a specific date?

Whenever a family comes to me for counseling, one of the facets of family life I look at is the amount of time the parents and children spend together. I have the parents take out their book of appointments and take a long look at their schedule. Have they been missing key events in their children's lives more often than not? Have they really given their child a sense that they are as important as their work schedule, or is there a hidden message of unavailability that they might not be meaning to convey?

—Richard

If you don't see any hope for change in your family routine or your child is exhibiting prolonged sadness or depression, it may be time to seek professional help. Consider taking yourself, your child and the problem to a qualified children's therapist.

5
OUT FOR THE EVENING

When one of us is gone for the evening, it really helps to scramble up the routine a little. If the kids are doing an activity they haven't done before, the evening goes by much more quickly and the hole left by our absence is less noticeable. I made a bedtime video for my three-year-old when I had to be out of town. It only took me fifteen minutes to make, but it made me feel better about leaving him, and he got a kick out of it even after I came home.

—*Joanna*

Lots of things can draw you away from home in the evening. Maybe it's a last minute push for completion of a project, a night class, a board meeting or traveling out-of-town on business. Whatever the cause, being absent in the evening means you miss out on the time when your family is generally at home eating dinner, doing homework, watching TV and simply hanging out. This chapter will show you ways to keep those evenings running smoothly without you.

MISSING DINNER

Sitting down and having dinner together at the table is a big thing for us when we are all together. When my husband is gone for dinner, it is a much

looser affair. The children and I sit at the breakfast bar in the kitchen and eat
something simple. It works well for us.

—Jeannie

Meals may not be formal occasions at your house, but most families have a routine of sorts worked out among themselves. Breakfast might be a frenzied affair with everyone grabbing what he or she needs; lunch may be spent with co-workers and classmates; dinners may be more organized with the entire family at the table. Even if your family eats dinner grazing out of the refrigerator, your presence is most likely to be missed at this mealtime.

WHEN THE CHIEF COOK IS GONE UNEXPECTEDLY

If you are the family cook as well, there will definitely be a gap to fill if you are away. The best approach is to make sure to have something that can be pulled out on a moment's notice if you are unable to make it home for dinner. The adult at home can always order pizza, but your children will probably get a kick out of it if your magic touch appears somewhere in the meal.

DINNER TWISTS

- Have on hand all the makings for pizza—there are lots of pizza kits with all the ingredients in one package. The adult at home can let the kids make the meal.

- Go to the grocery store ahead of time and let the children pick out all the food for a future evening meal. They will look forward to the meal with anticipation. When you can't make it home for dinner, let the adult at home help them prepare the meal they picked out.

- Buy a box of ice cream, popsicles or favorite dessert for the adult at home to present as a gift from you.

- Tell your family not to prepare dinner on a particular night and arrange for take-out food to be delivered to the door. Prepay the bill or leave

WORKING PARENTS, HAPPY KIDS

money to cover it, and be sure to tell the adult at home what you have arranged to do. Otherwise, the delivery person may be making a delivery to an empty house!

- Precook a favorite meal for the family and have it all ready for them to pop into the oven or into a serving dish. Be sure the adult at home lets the children know that you prepared the meal especially for them.

- Make a **Magic Meal Box** to be pulled out whenever you, the adult at home, or your children need it most. See below for instructions.
  - Get a box which will fit into one of your kitchen cupboards. Tell your family that this is going to be the **Magic Meal Box** and spend some time one evening decorating the box. Talk with your family about what kinds of mealtime foods and activities they would like to include in the box. Some sample items are:
    —Take-out menus from your favorite restaurants
    —Coupons for favorite restaurants or take-out items
    —Cash to pay for meal deliveries
    —The ingredients for an entire dinner
    —Leftover decorations, party hats, plates, cups and napkins from any parties
    —Whistles, gags, funny straws, magic tricks or anything which might be fun to take out at the dinner table to lighten the mood
    —Bags of chips, special chocolates, or any other favorite treats
    —Poems, jokes or stories to be read at the dinner table
    —Photographs which can be passed around
    —Fortune cookies
    —Chopsticks
    —Notes referring to meals in the refrigerator or freezer which you have bought or prepared ahead of time
  - Encourage each family member to sneak special items into the **Magic Meal Box** for the next time it is used. Everyone will have fun trying to catch each other, and when the box is pulled out for a meal, you can take turns guessing who put in each new item.

THE OCCASIONAL OR UNEXPECTED ABSENCE

When you are absent from a meal only occasionally, it can be fun to help make your family's dinner one to remember. Have your partner or caregiver surprise the kids with an unusual approach to their mealtime which will distract them from concentrating on your absence. These activities are for your children, but remember to consult with your partner or caregiver at home about which activities will be the most enjoyable (and manageable) for them as well.

DINNERTIME ACTIVITIES FOR AN OCCASIONAL ABSENCE

- Change the seating arrangement at the dining table. Have everyone sit at a different place and act like each other.

- Make dinner a picnic in the living room. The adult at home can spread out a sheet or tablecloth on the floor, use paper plates, cups and napkins and serve dinner picnic-style. If your children are small, they can bring some of their stuffed animal "friends" with them to the picnic. Have picnic "talk" like "Boy, are these mosquitoes bad!" to get the children laughing and joining in.

- If the weather is nice, take dinner to a park or outside in the backyard.

- The adult at home can surprise them with a visit to a special restaurant on the spur of the moment.

- Have a backwards supper—everyone at home can eat some dessert first.

- Everyone can think up a silly costume and wear it to the meal.

- Have breakfast foods for dinner—everyone can have their favorites.

- They all can grab something quick to eat and then go to the movies.

- The children can make place cards and place mats for everyone who will be at the meal and decide where everyone will sit.

Books for Young Children
Is This My Dinner? by Irma Simonton Black
Let's Eat by Gyo Fujikawa

Mom's Night Out by Julie Barbato
The Magic Porridge Pot by Paul Galdone
Pizza for Breakfast by Maryann Kovalski

ROUTINE OR LONG-TERM ABSENCES

I would make up weeks of dinner menus and have all the ingredients on hand for the woman who stayed with the kids. She told me she couldn't really cook, but if I gave her specific instructions, she did just fine 99% of the time.
—Heidi

If your dinnertime absences are a regular occurrence, you may want to take a different approach. Help your family set up a routine for the times you will not be there. They can pick out activities that they enjoy and reserve them for the times you will be gone. That way, they will have a whole set of dinnertime routines that they look forward to when you can't be there.

DINNERTIME ACTIVITIES FOR REGULAR ABSENCES

• They can try any of the ideas in **Dinnertime Activities for An Occasional Absence** on page 74.

• They can visit different and unusual restaurants until your family finds one or two they enjoy. They should visit these restaurants only when you are gone.

• You can leave special dinnertime messages for each member of the family on a cassette recorder, paper, the computer or whatever. (See the chapter on **Building the Lines of Communication** which starts on page 29 for more ideas.)

• The children can select the entire menu for the meal. If the adult at home has lots of energy, let them help prepare it. They might want to pick one particular meal that becomes a tradition each time the parent is away.

• If you are on a trip, your family can try to eat the foods you are eating. The adult at home can try to prepare a meal or order food from a restaurant that serves dishes similar to what you are eating. Or the family could visit a restaurant that serves the same kind of food. When you talk to your family, tell them about the special foods of the area you are visiting. If you are in the same region as your family, tell them what you had for dinner the night before and they can try to duplicate it.

Some examples are:
- Southern food: fried chicken, bar-b-q, gumbo
- Southwestern food: Mexican
- Northeastern food: baked beans, corned beef and cabbage, clam chowder
- Midwestern food: good old home cooking such as meat loaf, deviled eggs, or strawberry shortcake
- Northwestern food: salmon or other seafood
- International food: If your family can't find a restaurant that serves food from your destination, describe it and they can try to prepare something like it at home.

THE HOMEWORK BEAT

Many families in my practice struggle with the homework issue. Sometimes their children don't do the homework, sometimes they do it and don't hand it in. A homework checklist can help organize these children. Kids work really well on schedules. It helps if there is a dependable pattern after dinner and/or after school, and the schedule should be kept consistent whether the parent is there or not.

—Richard

Maintaining the homework routine presents a unique problem. If two people share the homework responsibilities, your absence can be filled by the other adult. Many families, however, have one parent who acts as the homework police for the children. Their job is to see that homework is done and that the children get the necessary help to do it, and they alone know each child's homework strengths and weaknesses.

If you are the normal "on-duty homework cop," you know that

each night's "beat" can consist of either a relatively uneventful patrol, or some major "criminal" behavior. When you are unable to be there, the whole system can break down. A few prior arrangements can do wonders in keeping the kids on task and helping the other adult fill in on your usual "beat."

WHEN THE HOMEWORK COP IS GONE UNEXPECTEDLY

- The first thing to do is to make sure the adult at home knows about the current homework situation. Clue them in on any homework routine you follow. Let them in on any tips you have discovered and prepare them for the traps: unmotivated kids; a difficult assignment; daydreamers or master procrastinators.

- If at all possible, talk directly to your children. Tell them you will not be there that night to assist with their homework. If there is time, discuss what they want to accomplish that night and wish them well. Be sure to remind them that someone will help them if they need it.

- Make sure the adult at home knows the teacher(s) and feels free to call them with a question. Fill out the **School Contacts** sheet on the next page and keep it in a handy place.

- If your child has tutors or special education teachers during or after school, make sure the adult at home knows what the drill is for any special approaches to homework. If they have assignments from these teachers unrelated to their regular school work, help the adult at home with any training they need prior to working with your child.

- Make sure you have a ready stash of stickers or small treats and have the adult at home give one of them to your child when he or she finishes all their homework.

- If you know that your child has a big test the next day and you can squeeze a minute or two from work, call them and ask them how it is going. If they are frustrated, help them brainstorm how they can get the job done. If they want to be quizzed, either quiz them over the phone or ask the adult with them to give a practice test.

School Contacts

Child:_____

Teacher: _____ Phone: _____

Teacher: _____ Phone: _____

Tutor: _____ Phone: _____

Classmate: _____ Phone: _____

Child:_____

Teacher: _____ Phone: _____

Teacher: _____ Phone: _____

Tutor: _____ Phone: _____

Classmate: _____ Phone: _____

Child:_____

Teacher: _____ Phone: _____

Teacher: _____ Phone: _____

Tutor: _____ Phone: _____

Classmate: _____ Phone: _____

Child:_____

Teacher: _____ Phone: _____

Teacher: _____ Phone: _____

Tutor: _____ Phone: _____

Classmate: _____ Phone: _____

Staying in the Homework Loop

For some parents, seeing homework papers coming in and out of the house is the only way they have of following their child's progress in school. If you are working marathon hours or are out of town, you can quickly feel completely in the dark where their school work is concerned. This can be frustrating. Try these suggestions for staying connected with what is happening at your child's school.

Managing Schoolwork from a Distance

- Notify your child's teachers when you anticipate working long hours or being out of town. This helps them to understand any behavioral changes in your child as well as letting them know who is in charge in your absence.

- If it's practical, have your children fax you homework papers they have completed or received back from the teacher. They can also fax you assignments they have not yet turned in for your proofreading and/or comments.

- If you are working late nights, use **Communication Central** (described on page 53) to pass papers back and forth. When you come home late, look in their school envelope, then write them a quick note about their work. They can read their "mail" from you when they get up in the morning.

- If you will be gone so long that your child's envelope in **Communication Central** will be overflowing, buy a large envelope or file folder for them to preserve homework papers while you are gone. After your return, make a date to go through the file folder together.

- If you anticipate a child attaining a special goal during your absence such as completing a spelling list, project or term paper, you can have a congratulatory packet prepared which the adult at home can present to the child when they achieve their goal. A sample packet might include any of the following:
  - A certificate of achievement
  - A handwritten note of congratulations or a taped message for their cassette recorder

- A handmade coupon for a treat or a favorite outing redeemable upon your return
- A balloon to blow up
- A special present the child has been working for

- If you have the time and the money, call your child and ask them to go over spelling words on the phone or listen to them practice their reading.

- If you know that they are doing a report on a particular topic, take a short trip to the library and gather a couple of books or articles pertaining to their topic. Present them as a contribution to their assignment.

USING A HOMEWORK CHECKLIST FOR BUSINESS TRIPS

The next time you have to leave town, take a checklist of your child's homework assignments with you. Sit down with each child before you leave and map out the assignments they know are coming due during the time you will be away. When it is complete, make a copy of the checklist for yourself and the adult at home.

The adult at home can use the checklist to prepare for any large assignments that might be coming due so no one will be caught off guard the night before the due date. You can take your copy with you as a reminder of what they should be working on during your absence. A phone call a night or two before a big assignment is due can give them a needed nudge to get busy.

HOMEWORK CHECKLIST

CHILD'S NAME: _____ DATE: _____

ASSIGNMENTS DUE:

	Subject	Assignment	Due Date	Help Needed
☐	_____	_____	_____	_____
☐	_____	_____	_____	_____
☐	_____	_____	_____	_____
☐	_____	_____	_____	_____
☐	_____			

MATERIALS NEEDED TO COMPLETE THESE ASSIGNMENTS:

☐ _____
☐ _____
☐ _____
☐ _____
☐ _____
☐ _____

PROBLEMS ANTICIPATED: _____
_____
_____

WHO CAN HELP OUT IF I GET STUCK:

Classmate: _____ Phone: _____
Classmate: _____ Phone: _____
Teacher: _____ Phone: _____
Teacher: _____ Phone: _____

MISSING OUT ON FAMILY TV TIME

My kids and I have a ritual of watching a specific nightly TV show. Cuddling up on my bed each night for our show gives us both entertainment and some precious downtime in our busy lives. We even refer to the show in our daily conversations and jokes. When we are away from each other at night, I watch the show if I can. I know they are watching it and it's a way for me to share in their lives when we are not together. I also know that I will be able to join in the conversations when I get back home.

—Pati

Some families have specific TV shows that everyone enjoys watching. Some families have TV rituals, like making popcorn, lying on the floor, or cuddling on the couch together. Actually watching the show is part of the fun, but coming together as a family is what's really important. You don't have to miss out on this ritual entirely when you are gone.

FAMILY TV TIME ACTIVITIES FOR YOU AND YOUR CHILDREN

- Preserve your family routine by asking your family to tape the show and wait until you get home so you can all watch it in your usual way.

- If you are traveling, watch the show in your hotel room, then call your children and talk about the episode you both just watched.

- Ask one of your children to tape the show for you while they watch it. Then you can watch it when you have time. See **Recording a TV Show on Our VCR** on page 83.

- When you view the recorded show, make some popcorn or get out a special treat. The aroma may entice a family member or two to watch it again.

- Ask your child(ren) to watch the show carefully and then bring you up-to-date when you get home. Tell them they can show you what happened any way they want—stories, acting it out, or drawing pictures.

Children—if they are old enough—often enjoy having a responsibility like being in charge of videotaping the show for you. If they don't know how to run the VCR, teach them. You will be giving your child another way to do a favor for someone else in the family and also be instilling a little bit of independence in them at the same time.

RECORDING A TV SHOW ON OUR VCR

Name of Show: _____

Date It Is On: _____/_____/_____   Time It Is On: _____

Channel: _____   Length of Show: _____

VCR Plus+ Code:_____

How to Record on our VCR:

1. _____

2. _____

3. _____

4. _____

BEDTIME BONDS FROM A DISTANCE

I made a bedtime video for my kids and it has resulted in one of the more comical aspects of my shared visitation. I made it for my children to watch when I was working out-of-town. Apparently, it turned into a frequently watched "show" at their dad's house. While driving to school one day, my eleven-year-old announced to me that Dad was getting pretty sick of seeing and hearing me at his house all the time!

—Pati

Bedtime is a period when your children might miss you the most. An effective strategy for your absence is to develop a new bedtime routine which preserves as much of their familiar routine as possible.

USING A BEDTIME VIDEO

One way to combat your children's potential anxieties is for you to make an interactive bedtime video which will keep you as part of their bedtime routine. It's fun for the children, and lightens the nighttime tasks for the parent at home.

The point of the video is to include as much of your children's bedtime routine as you can. You can be filmed sitting on a bed or a couch reading bedtime stories, or you can have someone film you walking through the house reminding your children about the different parts of their bedtime routine. Stop at the bathroom and say, "I hope you haven't forgotten to use your mouthwash. Remember how I have to remind you to do it? Well, here I am!" The more interactive the video is, the more involved the children will get.

End each video with a special message for each child about how much you love them and miss them. For those of you without a video camera, recording the same routine on a cassette tape also brings your warmth and love into your home. Using this approach can provide new motivation for getting ready for bed in a timely fashion.

It can sound intimidating to make a video, but it only takes 20 or 30 minutes to make the tape from start to finish. Once it is done, it can be used again and again. Borrow a video camera and either get someone to film you carrying out the bedtime routine or position the camera on a tripod and film the sequence yourself.

BEDTIME VIDEO BASICS

- Plan what you want to include in your video. The typical components are :
  - Greeting
  - Getting the children ready for bed:
    —getting on their pajamas
  —brushing their teeth and any dental hygiene routine they follow
  —washing their faces
  —going to the bathroom
  —grabbing their favorite blanket, pillow, stuffed animal or doll
  - Reading or telling them a story
  - Wishing them each a personal good night

- If you don't think you'll remember what you want to say, jot some reminders down on a card to keep by you when you record the tape.

- Pick out the story or stories you wish to read or tell for your bedtime video.

- If you don't have them already, borrow a video camera and a tripod. If you can't find a tripod, experiment with propping the camera on a stool or table with books on it.

- Start the camera and go for it. Don't worry about goofing up or saying the wrong thing—there are no mistakes possible. Sometimes, the more "homemade" it is, the better your children will enjoy it.

- Read the story slowly and clearly. Make comments about the pictures or the characters in the book. You can hold the book up to the camera so that the children can see the pages.

If you are stuck for ideas on what to say in the video, we have provided a sample script below. Be sure to talk to each child personally during the taping. It *really* is much easier to make a tape than it may sound. Some children continue to watch the bedtime video tapes after the parent has come home. You might later consider filming an actual bedtime routine with the kids. After the novelty of the first tape has worn off, seeing themselves on the TV screen on this second tape will spark their interest again.

SAMPLE SCRIPT FOR A BEDTIME VIDEO

"Hi Adam, hi Sarah. I sure do wish I was sitting with you right now instead of working. I especially hate it when I miss seeing each of you off to bed. One of my favorite parts of our bedtime routine is reading you a story and talking about our day.

"I don't want to miss out just because I am not there, so _____ (*insert caregiver/partner's name*) is going to help me out tonight with your bedtime.

"OK, the first thing I want everybody to do is go get on your pajamas. _____ will pause the VCR and I will wait for you to get them on and come back. I wonder who will get back first."

The adult at home pauses the VCR and helps the kids get dressed for bed.

"Good job. Sarah, are you wearing your pink nightgown, and Adam, are you wearing your big blue tee shirt? Now it's time to brush your teeth and go to the bathroom. Adam, be sure to brush those back teeth like the dentist told you to, and Sarah, don't forget to use that new pink mouthwash. Oh, and when you come back, bring your pillows. Sarah, you might also want to bring Nanny Bear."

Once again, the VCR is paused and the kids complete getting ready for bed. The adult can help them gather their favorite stuffed animals, dolls or blankets. While the kids are in the bathroom is a good time to locate the books that are going to be read, so there won't have to be a massive search effort for them later.

"Great job! Your teeth look super. OK, everybody, get comfortable, because here we go.

"On this tape, I'm going to read _____ and _____. If you want to follow along with the stories, I put the books right next to the VCR when I left. If you have been looking at them, tell _____ where they are and she can help you gather them. I'll wait while you find them."

Make some comments about each story as you read it. If your children have favorite parts, mention them. The more you can say each child's name on the tape, the more attention they'll feel they got.

"Well, I hope you liked the stories. It's time for bed now, so I am going to wish you a very special good night. _____ is going to take you into your rooms now to go to sleep."

Insert any special rituals, words, or bedtime phrases you and your children share here. Also include a personal message to each child.

"Now I am going to send you my good night kisses and hugs. OK, send some back to me, now. Wow!!, I felt that one. Come on now, Adam, I want a kiss from you. I sure do love you both."

The role the bedtime video plays in your children's lives may be constantly changing. At first, they may want to watch it every night. They may want to get the books and read along or sit in front of it and listen. If you travel frequently, you may consider making a new tape every couple of months and building up a bedtime video library. Your children can then choose a favorite to watch before bed.

Don't be dismayed if your children choose not to watch the video for a time. There might be several things going on here. They could be bored and it could be time to make a new video; they could be angry at you and this could be their way of fighting back; or they could simply be more excited about a story or other bedtime activity. Don't take it personally. Ask them if they want a new video, or if they have any ideas on how you can be a part of their bedtime when you have to work.

THE PERSONAL "GOOD NIGHT" TAPE

Our neighbor, Kristin—who has become a wonderful part of our family—was always looking for ways to say "Good Night" to my son—her "adopted" brother. When he was about three or four, she started a "Good Night" tape for him on his cassette player, then added 30 seconds or so onto it each day. Sometimes she sang a song, sometimes she talked about things that had happened that day, or sometimes she just said, "I love you." She would place the cassette player next to his pillow after she had recorded her message, and he could hardly wait to get into bed that night. He would rewind the tape and listen to all the previous good night messages, then squeal with delight as he heard the newly recorded one. That tape became one of his most special possessions at the time.

—Joanna

The section on **Taping Love Messages on a Cassette Player** on page 34 discusses the idea of children having personal cassette players. If your children do, it's a snap to custom-make a good night message for each of them. Label a tape *(their name)*'s **GOOD NIGHT TAPE**, press the record button, and just start talking. Sing a song, tell a favorite story, and then give your child a good night message. When they climb into bed, they can pop the tape in and listen to it. It will be theirs and theirs alone prepared by you.

Each of these techniques can show your children that you truly do miss being there in person. Use these and some of the ones mentioned in **Building the Lines of Communication** beginning on page 29 to keep your love an integral part of their bedtime routine.

 Books for Young Children
Close Your Eyes by Jean Marzollo
Good Night Moon by Margaret Wise Brown
Night Again by Karla Kuskin
Ten, Nine, Eight by Molly Bang
Time for Bed, the Babysitter Said by Peggy Perry Anderson
Aunt Nina, Good Night by Franz Brandenburg

One bedtime routine that we started a long time ago was a nightly bedtime story. Instead of reading or making a new one up each night, we started a serial story that has been going on for years. The characters are Winnie-the-Pooh, his cousin, Glennie, and the monkey, Peanut. Each night we would review what had happened the previous night, then add parts to the story. I would mostly tell the story, but the kids would ask questions, and suggest things. They are now nine and eleven and they still ask to continue the story every so often. It would have been great if we had put that on tape so the kids could listen to it when I was gone.

—Jan

6
OFF ON A TRIP

When I travel, I call them. I try to find out what they are doing and I remark on things I know they had scheduled. I stick a pin in the map before I leave to show them where I am. I take a lot of photos and bring back trinkets. I always take pictures of the kids I see when I travel. My kids are curious about the other kids. They want to know their names, how old they are, and what they do for fun. When I return, I go over the pictures with them.

—Doug

Business travel is definitely a mixed bag. If you don't travel often, you probably greet each trip as a "bonus" vacation and count the days until you leave. You look forward to the leisurely dinners, uninterrupted telephone conversations and having the flexibility to work and play with no other responsibilities tugging at you. If you travel regularly, however, it can be more of a grind, and it's often harder to leave everyone. You may dread more lonely nights of channel surfing, eating alone in restaurants and waves of homesickness.

No matter how you view your business travel, you probably find your thoughts drifting back to your children while you are away. Do you wonder if their homework is getting done, and if they are getting to bed at a decent hour? If one of your children missed you acutely during your last trip, do you find yourself wondering how it is going this time? If your trip interferes with a special event at school or a family celebration, do you yearn to be back home to participate in the goings-on?

The purpose of this chapter is to help you develop a **Trip Routine** for your family. What's a **Trip Routine**? It's a set of unique activities that each member of your family follows before you leave, while you are gone, and after your trip is over. Try one or two activities each time you travel and your family will soon develop its own trip routine. Then, when you announce that you are going on a trip, instead of the grunts and groans you usually get, your children will know they have something to look forward to while you are away.

When I go up to Prudhoe Bay to work, I work a minimum of 12 hours a day—more like 14 or 15. I live in the same place I work and it is institutional living. It's not really a resort or hotel situation. I work seven days on and then have a week off. Keeping the family together in spirit takes a lot of energy. Having rituals for my departure and my arrival helps me save my energy for the important things. Without rituals, my house is chaos when I leave and chaos when I come home.

—Candi

➤

USING *GROUND CONTROL CENTER* TO STAY CONNECTED

A good place to start in developing your **Trip Routine** is to make a *Ground Control Center.* As a traveling parent, your destinations separate you from your children. Building a *Ground Control Center* in your house will allow you and your family to use your travel destinations as a connecting link to one another. A *Ground Control Center* is not an elaborate system. It is simply a place in the house where your children can gather around calendars and maps to discuss you and your destinations while following the course of your trip.

Your *Ground Control Center* can be either a permanent or temporary addition to your house. If you travel frequently, it might be good to leave it in place. If travel is less frequent, you can roll up the banner, maps and decorations and tuck them away until the next trip is scheduled.

SETTING UP *GROUND CONTROL CENTER*

Don't panic! You can set up a ***Ground Control Center*** easily and quickly. By collecting the materials detailed below, you will have a place in your home where your children can learn about where you are and when you will be coming home. It will also be a place where they can feel in touch with you while you are away. Here's a list of the supplies you will need.

MATERIALS FOR THE *GROUND CONTROL CENTER*

- A bin, box or basket

- This book

- Maps of your state, the United States and/or the world–depending upon where you travel

- An atlas—preferably one suited to your children's age level

- Removable map stickers or push pins to identify locations on the maps

- A calendar

MATERIALS FOR MAKING **COUNTING CARDS**— IF YOU HAVE YOUNG CHILDREN WHO DON'T USE CALENDARS

- Paper or poster board—bright colors make it look festive

- Scissors

- Pen or colored markers

- Hole punch

- Push pins or tape

BUILDING *GROUND CONTROL CENTER*

Once you've gathered all the materials, follow these step-by-step instructions:

- Find a spot on the wall and either pin or hang up the state, U.S. and/or world maps—depending upon the traveler's destinations.

- If you have young children who do not understand using calendars, design and make **Counting Cards.** You can make a deck in fifteen minutes or you can set aside an hour for it to be a family activity. These **Counting Cards** will be hung on the wall in the *Ground Control Center* to represent the number of nights you will be away from home, so decide on the maximum number of nights you will be away and make that many **Counting Cards.**

1. Divide an 8 1/2" by 11" sheet of paper into four equal pieces by drawing lines or folding. Each section should measure 4 1/4" by 5 1/2".
2. Cut on the lines or folds. Continue doing this until you have sixteen cards. This will take four sheets of paper. If you know you will always be away for less than two weeks at a time, you could make only four, eight or twelve cards.
3. Take your marker, crayon or pen and—in big, bold numerals— number a card **1**, the next card **2**, the next card **3** and so on until you have numbered all the cards.
4. To further reinforce the idea of what each number represents, place the appropriate number of stickers on each of the cards to give a visual representation of the number. For example, put one apple sticker on the **1** card, two horse stickers on the **2** card, and continue until you get to your highest number.
5. If you are going to hang them up on the wall, punch a hole in the top center of each card.

6. Use push pins to hang the cards in **Ground Control Center**. Make sure you have extra tape if you are taping the cards up. Now they're ready to go!

- Get the bin, box or basket and place in it: this book, the calendar and/or **Counting Cards** depending upon the age of your children, your atlas, the map stickers, and push pins or tape for the **Counting Cards**.

- Make your **Ground Control Center** look official by decorating it.
  - Pin or hang cutouts from maps or magazine pictures of faraway destinations. Have your children give it their personal touch by decorating it with their own pictures of airplanes, earth and places they would like to visit or whatever comes to their minds.
  - Make a banner with **Ground Control Center** on it or a name of your choosing. Use your desktop publishing software if you have a computer or tape sheets of paper together. Use markers, glitter, stickers, crayons and whatever else your family likes.
  - Decorate the bin or box with pictures from magazines, original creations or cutouts from maps.

GROUND CONTROL CENTER ACTIVITIES FOR YOUR FAMILY

Inaugurate your **Ground Control Center** with a few family activities. These can be tried at any time. You will be amazed to find out how much your children can learn about geography and the world around them by hanging out at the **Ground Control Center**.

STATE, U.S. AND WORLD MAP ACTIVITIES

- Mark all the places the family has visited.

- Mark all the places where friends or family members are living now.

- Mark all the places that family members were born.

- Pick out five countries in the morning newspaper and find them on the world map.

- Explain the legend on the map to your children. Tell them about scale and how one inch represents a much larger area. Using the information you told them about the legend and scale, measure and figure out the distances between the following points:

Your city and New York City: _____ miles
Your city and Disney World (Orlando, FL): _____ miles
Your city and Anchorage, Alaska: _____ miles
Your city and Washington, D.C.: _____ miles

- Explain the time zones on the U.S. and World maps. If they are not on the map, draw them in or find a picture with them on it. There is usually a time zone map for the U.S. in your telephone directory.

- Figure out what time it is in the following places. What are people likely to be doing there right now?

Your city: _____ Time now: _____
Honolulu, Hawaii Time now: _____
Boston, Massachusetts Time now: _____
Houston, Texas Time now: _____

- Make a list of all the people you know in each U.S. time zone other than your own. Guess what these people might be doing right now.

PREPARING FOR YOUR TRIP

My older son just does not like surprises. He likes lots of warning before any changes in his routine—even going out to dinner. If one of us is going out of town, we need to start telling him well before the event so he doesn't get thrown for a loop when it's time for one of us to leave. Now that he is older, it doesn't take much—a look at the calendar every day and a reminder here and there. If we take the time to prepare him, we can sail out the door without a worry.
—Joanna

Everyone in your household—you, your partner or caregiver, and your children—need warning as to when you will be leaving. It may be for different reasons, but you all need to mentally prepare for your trip. It can be especially upsetting to a young child to return home from school or daycare and find out that Mommy or Daddy is gone and will not be there to put them to bed at night. A **Pre-trip Countdown** helps the whole family prepare for your trip, and it makes an ideal start to your **Trip Routine**. Children—especially young ones—benefit from a **Pre-trip Countdown** because when you do leave, they are not taken by surprise. They don't need lots of preparation. A two or three day notice is usually ideal.

THE PRE-TRIP COUNTDOWN

- Decide how much warning your child needs—one, two or three days.

- If you decide that a two-day warning is appropriate, pull out the **Counting Cards** numbered **1** and **2**. (See **Building *Ground Control Center*** on page 92.) Two days before you leave on your trip, go with your child to the ***Ground Control Center*** and hang or tape the cards up. Explain to your child that each night at bedtime, one of the cards will be removed. When the numbers are gone, you will be leaving on your trip the following day.

- It may also be useful—especially if there are older children in your family—to get out a calendar and mark the day you are leaving and the day you will be returning home.

- When you remove the last card the night before you leave, give your child a brief description about where you are going and what you will be doing on your trip. Reassure them that you will remain in touch with them and briefly mention some of the ways you will do it— phone calls, faxes, postcards, e-mail or letters. If you are leaving on a late night flight, it is especially important to tell your child that you will not be there when they awaken in the morning.

- This is also the ideal time to give them some idea of when you will be coming home. See **Saying Goodbye on the Eve of Your Departure...** on page 99 for a good strategy.

Opening the Channels of Communication

Before you leave, make sure the lines of communication with your children will be up and running while you are gone. Read the chapter **Building the Lines of Communication** which starts on page 29 for ideas about inventive ways to keep in touch. Pick one new communication activity to try each time you travel until you have a host of family favorites for your **Trip Routine**. It doesn't matter how open the communication channels are if no one knows where to reach you! Copy the itinerary worksheet on the next page and fill it out. Post it in *Communication Central* (see pages 53-58) or the *Ground Control Center*.

Packing Your Bags

When my husband packs for a trip, the kids sometimes write him little notes and try to sneak them into his suitcase. Sometimes he writes notes back to them and hides them in the house.

—*Jeannie*

Even if your children don't help, packing can afford you an excellent opportunity for setting up a special trip ritual. It can also give you and your children a way to set up communication channels to activate while you are on the trip. Check out the following activities and see if any of them strike a chord for your family.

Packing Activities for Your Children

- Give your child a suitcase and let them "pack" for an imaginary trip.

- Ask your child to pack their school backpack or daycare duffel bag for the next day while you pack.

- Let them cut out a construction paper suitcase or cut it out for them

WHERE I CAN BE
REACHED ON MY TRIP

Day _____: _____/_____/_____

Traveling to _____: by ❑ car ❑ plane ❑ train

    Route or Flight: _____ Phone: _____

    Staying at: _____ Phone: _____

    Contact there: _____ Phone: _____

Day _____: _____/_____/_____

Traveling to _____: by ❑ car ❑ plane ❑ train

    Route or Flight: _____ Phone: _____

    Staying at: _____ Phone: _____

    Contact there: _____ Phone: _____

Day _____: _____/_____/_____

Traveling to _____: by ❑ car ❑ plane ❑ train

    Route or Flight: _____ Phone: _____

    Staying at: _____ Phone: _____

    Contact there: _____ Phone: _____

Day _____: _____/_____/_____

Traveling to _____: by ❑ car ❑ plane ❑ train

    Route or Flight: _____ Phone: _____

    Staying at: _____ Phone: _____

    Contact there: _____ Phone: _____

Day _____: _____/_____/_____

Traveling to _____: by ❑ car ❑ plane ❑ train

    Route or Flight: _____ Phone: _____

    Staying at: _____ Phone: _____

    Contact there: _____ Phone: _____

ahead of time. Give them several magazines and catalogs and let them "pack" their suitcase by cutting out pictures of items they want to take on their trip. Select several destinations and notice how the items they pack change. Some suggested destinations are:
- a week at the beach in Hawaii or the South Pacific
- a mountain climbing expedition to Mount Everest, Kilimanjaro or a mountain near you
- a visit to a favorite relative or friend
- a trip to see a landmark or tourist attraction your child is interested in
- a trip to Disney World, Sea World, Epcot Center, Universal Studios or Splash Mountain

- Ask them to make a surprise cassette tape to tuck in your suitcase. Ask them to sing a song, tell you about their favorite things, or get as silly as they want on the tape.

- If you keep a journal, ask your children to write a special message which you will read when you reach your destination. Don't forget to leave a message in their journal.

- Ask each of your children to pick out a small item to take with you as a remembrance of them. Let them select it and place it in your suitcase. They can "wrap up" the item in paper towels or tissue paper as a surprise for you. Some ideas are:
- a picture of them
- a small toy
- a little stuffed animal
- a picture they drew

PACKING REMEMBRANCES

You certainly don't need any time-consuming, extra activities in addition to the chore of packing, but these quick activities are worth the little time they take. They will leave a little piece of you behind and they will let your child know that you will be thinking of them while you are gone.

Packing Activities for You

• Pick out something of yours for your child to keep until you return. Take into account whether they will want to sleep with it when you select the item. The item need not be fancy—the more it reminds them of you, the better it is.

Some suggestions are:
- An article of clothing that you wear a lot
- A photograph of you and your child together
- A piece of jewelry
- Your slippers
- Your pillow

• Show your children a family photograph you are planning to display in your hotel room. If you have the time and energy, help them pick out a photograph to send along with you.

SAYING GOODBYE
ON THE EVE OF YOUR DEPARTURE...

We talk about him leaving on a trip before he goes, but it still sometimes takes them by surprise. "What do you mean Daddy's leaving today?" they might say. It doesn't really throw them for a loop, though, because his going on trips is so much a part of our normal routine. Now that he is traveling internationally, his trips are going to be longer—two or three weeks at a time. That is going to be harder for all of us.

—Jeannie

You can do your whole family a big service by helping your children understand when exactly you will be back. That is easily done by using the **Counting Cards** and the techniques used in **The Pre-trip Countdown** on page 95. Your children and the adult at home will use the cards to count down the nights you are away from home. That way, when your children are desperate to know when you will be back, there is a visual way to clue them in.

Departure's Eve Activities for You and Your Children

- On the night before you go away or on the morning of your departure, count out the numbered cards that represent the number of nights you will be away. You can also make a chain of paper rings for the appropriate number.

- With your children beside you, hang the cards in the **Ground Control Center**.

- Explain that each night you are away they can take down the card with the highest number, or remove one of the rings from the paper chain. When they take down the last card—the number 1—or remove the last paper ring, you will be home the very next day.

- If you have young children, remember to use examples that relate to your children's lives. You might try: "Each of these rings or cards is one of your nighttimes or big sleeps. When you go to bed each night, Nanny will help you remove one ring or card. After they are all gone, I will be home to tuck you in bed that night."

- In addition, show your children your destination the first night of your trip. Even if you are going to be in several different locations during your trip, show them only the first night's destination. If your children are older, you can tell them about your other destinations too, but don't mark them. They will be doing that while you are gone. (See **Tracking Your Trip** on page 104.)

- **Caution!!** Your children will literally be counting the days waiting for your return. They will be very disappointed if Mom or Dad does not return when they are expecting them. If there is a chance your schedule will change, you can call during the trip and have your family add or take away **Counting Cards** or paper chain rings. If you have frequent schedule changes, or you just can't be sure of your arrival day, you may want to eliminate this activity altogether.

Books for Young Children
Daddy and Ben Together by Miriam Stecher and Alice Kendall
That Summer Night by Charlotte Zolotow

My Mom Travels a Lot by Caroline Bauer
Don't Forget to Write by Martina Selway

If there is one thing I have learned over the years, it is that children need to watch their parent go out the door if it is at all possible. I know someone who used to try and save her son from getting upset by leaving quietly. He would look all over the house for her. It's only fair to the child. It also helps to make a ritual out of it.

—Heidi

DURING YOUR TRIP

Pati and I were at a conference in New Orleans once, and we decided to walk back to the hotel after dinner. It was just after Mardi Gras, and we happened to be walking along the route the Mardi Gras parade had taken just a few days earlier. As we walked, we noticed the remnants of the parade on the ground—colored metal coins and scores of beaded necklaces. We gathered the "loot" as we walked and arrived back at our hotel laden with the goods—which we plunked in our bathtub for a good washing. When we got back home, we had the best present anyone could bring three- and four-year-old boys—pirate treasure! That was six years ago, and the necklaces and "doubloons" have now been handed down to my second son for his treasure.

—Joanna

Your **Trip Routine** doesn't have to stop the minute you close the door behind you. You can help your children the most by actively communicating with them while you are gone (see **Building the Lines of Communication** which starts on page 29) and also by picking up some mementos of your trip for them.

GRABBING THE FREEBIES

One of the most popular things parents can do during a trip is to buy their child a present. Unfortunately these presents often turn out to be either overpriced or something that captures their child's attention for only a day or two. Instead, bring your child some of the free presents that surround you on every trip. They won't break the family pocketbook and there is a never ending supply of them.

The following list of freebies may not look like much to you, but children love using and playing with them. Give older children the items to use for their intended purposes. Younger children may find dozens of other uses for them in their creative play. These items are naturals for playing store and post office and they can make bath and play time fun for weeks after you arrive home.

FREEBIES FOR YOUR CHILDREN

- In Hotels
  - Toiletries such as: soaps, lotions, shampoos, tanning oils, and bath gelee
  - Sewing kits
  - Combs
  - Stationery
  - Laundry Bags
  - Shoe Shining Bags

- In Restaurants
  - Menus
  - Napkins
  - Drink garnish or hors d'oeuvres holders like swords or paper umbrellas

- In Airplane, Train or Bus Stations
  - Schedules
  - Baggage tags
  - In-flight magazines
  - Motion sickness bag

- If You Are Traveling Internationally:
  - Coins or currency
  - Brochures
  - Maps
  - Receipts

COUNTING THE DAYS UNTIL YOU RETURN

"When are you coming home?" is probably the most frequently asked question by the children of traveling moms and dads. While you are gone, the adult at home can help your children understand the answer to this question by using the *Ground Control Center* to count down the days until you return home. Older children may want to use their own personal calendar, but young children will probably get a kick out of marking off the days of your trip using the **Counting Cards** or the paper chain rings mentioned in **Saying Goodbye on the Eve of Your Departure** on page 99. Whenever a young child asks plaintively, "When is (Mommy or Daddy) coming home?", the adult at home now has a ready place to take them for the answer.

COUNTING THE DAYS ACTIVITIES FOR YOUR CHILDREN AND THE ADULT AT HOME

- Each night, the adult at home and the children all visit the *Ground Control Center*, remove one of the cards or rings, and then figure out how many nights are remaining in your trip.

- If there are young children, they can talk about what that number of days represents by relating it to their lives. For example, "In just three more nighttimes, your mommy will be home!" The adult at home can also use this activity as a springboard for teaching young children their numbers. Children can practice writing the appropriate number each night when they remove a card. Or they can look about the room and spot objects that represent the number: two candles, three books, and so on.

- Older children can use the family calendar or their own personal calendar to cross off the days.

- When the last card or ring is removed, the adult at home can tell the children that you will be home the very next day. She can talk about how you are getting home and what your travel plans are. She can tell them what time of day you will be arriving, but ask her to be general. Travel plans can change and planes can be delayed. Ask her to use terms like "We hope Mom/Dad will be home for dinner" if you have an afternoon arrival.

 Books for Young Children
Farm Counting Book by Jane Miller
A Number of Dragons by Loreen Leedy
1 is One by Tasha Tudor
One Was Johnny by Maurice Sendak
Helen Oxenbury's Numbers of Things by Helen Oxenbury
The Very Hungry Caterpillar by Eric Carle

TRACKING YOUR TRIP

Most people play the game, Where in the World is Carmen San Diego? Well we play, Where In the World is John Kreilkamp? He is starting to do a lot of international travel, so we go upstairs to the globe and give it a spin and figure out where he is that day. We talk about where he is and what he is having for dinner.

—Jeannie

In addition to counting down the days of your trip, your children can feel much more involved if they follow your travels. Your **Ground Control Center** is ideal for that. Each night, when they cross off a day or take down a counting card, they can track your trip as well. It is an ideal way for your children to learn a little about geography as well as to feel more connected to you.

The adult at home or an older child—the "Captain"—can be in charge of the **Trip Tracking Activities**. If you are a frequent traveler, you can appoint a different "Captain" each time you go away. Give the following list of activities to your "Captain" along with your itinerary when you leave on your next trip.

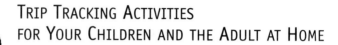

TRIP TRACKING ACTIVITIES FOR YOUR CHILDREN AND THE ADULT AT HOME

- Your children and the adult at home can mark your destination each night with a new sticker or push pin. If you haven't traveled that day, the children can put a new sticker or push pin next to the old one or just leave it alone.

- If your itinerary is up-in-the-air, you can fax, phone or e-mail your destinations as you arrive. When they find out where you are, your children can then mark it on the map.

- The adult at home and your children can talk about how you got to your destination, where you are staying, and what kinds of activities, meetings or schedule you will have there.

- Your children can try to figure out what time it is where you are. They can also try to guess what you are doing at that very moment.

- Your children can look in the newspaper to see what the weather is where you are.

- Your children can look in the atlas or encyclopedia for information about your current stop.

- If your travel is international, or in a different part of the country, they can ask you and then talk about the differences in food, people, languages and customs.

- The adult at home can surf the Internet or go to the library for additional information about your destination. She can ask the librarian to find age-appropriate books for each child.

- The adult at home can write down any questions your children have about the stops on your trip. They can ask you about them during your next phone call or when you return.

My eight-year-old had always heard the words "Prudhoe Bay," but as far as she knew, Prudhoe Bay was near the airport because that is where she would drop me off. She knew I got on an airplane and went away, but she had no idea how far I went and what I did when I got there. Showing her where we went on the map really made a difference. All of a sudden, she understood how far away I went. She finally understood why I just couldn't pop in every so often and give her a hug and a kiss.

—Candi

MISSING THE TRAVELER

My husband traveled a lot and I traveled some, so we didn't do anything special. Nine times out of ten, I would watch the kids when Kevin was gone and vice versa. So I guess we didn't feel like there was a loss. But there was. I would have a heck of a time with our younger son when Kevin was out of town. He would really act out. Had we done some of these things, I think it would have cut down on this behavior. I think a lot of times parents don't realize their kids are missing the other spouse. When I look back on these business trips, I am convinced it was the absence of Kevin or me which caused all these behavior problems in Jake. He was missing us. Some of these trips would last one or two weeks and, for a young child, this is a long time to be without Mom or Dad.

—Mary

Overnight trips may provoke feelings of loss, sadness and confusion in children—especially the young ones. Often these feelings cycle in and out of their behavior throughout your entire absence. Temper tantrums, crying jags, hypersensitivity and changes in sleeping and eating habits can all be signals that your child is missing you.

Try having the adult at home with your children read **Chasing Away Boredom and the Blues**, which starts on page 59, for ideas in helping your child cope with the stress of missing you. The **Boredom Buster Activities** starting on page 60 can be a great way to take their minds off your absence. If your child is old enough, why not include them in the choice of activity? You can sit down with them before you leave while they pick out activities that sound fun to them, or you can let the adult at home do that after you have gone. When the situation calls for more intervention, the **Bucking the Blues Activities** starting on page 66 have techniques for helping your child identify and gain control over their feelings. If your child is missing you consistently while you are away, you will want to try some of the activities before your next trip.

⟶

RETURNING HOME

We have no special routine for returning home. It used to be that we met their father at the gate with all the bells and whistles, but we don't do that anymore. It was really fun for the kids when they were younger. Now they usually have basketball or some type of activity, so we drive to the airport and pick him up at the baggage claim area when we can. Our family's needs have really changed in that way.

—Jeannie

Just as you had to prepare your child for your departure, a similar investment needs to be made for your return. The cards are all down in the **Ground Control Center** and the next destination on the map is home. You and your family are all filled with fantasies of a perfect reunion, but, as we all know, fantasies are not often what reality is made of.

In actuality, unless the trip was short, you often return exhausted. You land on the doorstep like a tired, bedraggled dog. The parent or caregiver lies in wait—ready to turn over the house and the kids to you so he or she can take a break. Your children are like coiled springs—ready to jump you and relate every event that has occurred during your absence in the first fifteen minutes you are home. This is the recipe for a disaster waiting to happen, and it doesn't have to be this way.

WHEN YOU RETURN EXHAUSTED

When I come home, I am too tired to just fall into the routine of keeping up with my kids' energy levels. Having rituals that help divert their attention when you come home makes all the difference in the world. When I returned this week, we got movies for my first night back. Instead of having to deal with each child's demands, we cuddled up on the couch and I got to relax. I think we will do that every time I come home now.

—Candi

If the trip has been a marathon of meetings and time zones, time for your recovery is definitely necessary. Try some of the transition ideas below to occupy your children and give you a chance to recuperate.

TRANSITION IDEAS FOR A WEARY TRAVELER AND THEIR FAMILY

- Spend a few hours with your family, and then ask your partner for a transition period while you recover from jet lag and the stress of travel. If you are using a caregiver, think about paying them to stay for an additional few hours or a day to help out at the end of your trip.

- Another option is to arrange for the children to be gone when you actually arrive home. This will give you a couple of hours to settle in before the kids overwhelm you with attention.

- Prepare the children. Tell your children that although you are home, you are very tired and will need lots of sleep and time to unwind. If your children are young, ask the adult at home to plan one more day of diversionary activities.

- Ask the adult at home to plan a simple meal for your first night at home. If the kids want to have a big celebration, request that it be postponed until the next night.

- Rent a family-oriented video or two that everyone can watch. Make popcorn and everyone can get cozy with quilts, blankets and pillows on the couch or floor. You can catnap if you need to during the movies.

- If you are exhausted, ask the adult at home to plan an activity outside of the home for the first night, like a movie out, a bike ride, a long walk or a visit with friends or relatives.

- While you rest, have your children put the finishing touches on journal entries, drawings or videos that they made for you.

WHEN YOU ARE REASONABLY RESTED

I just like to share memories of my trip with them. I might tell them about a funny person or an especially fussy baby on the plane. I'll come home and tell them, "You wouldn't believe what this person did on the plane today!" They get a kick out of those stories.

—*Jan*

If you are likely to be in pretty good shape when you return, encourage the adult at home to help your children get out the bells and whistles for a big welcome. They will have almost as much fun planning and preparing for the party as they will at the big event. Here are some ideas your children might like:

WELCOME HOME ACTIVITIES

- If it has been a long trip, your children can plan a welcome-home party. The adult at home can help them purchase some balloons and funny hats, and they can make a banner. Noisemakers can be fun if you are rested.

- Your children and the adult at home can devise a simple treasure hunt for you. The best treasure is something the kids made for you while you were away.

- They can decorate the room with big family posters—photos enlarged on a copy machine or pictures drawn by the children.

- They can create a restaurant at home for the first family meal. The kids can make placemats, menus and the adult at home can help them prepare and serve your favorite meal.

- All of you can make plans for a night out for the whole family with an activity everyone enjoys.

Easing Back to Normal

Just because your child isn't going crazy to see you at that moment doesn't mean that they don't love you. They might be watching their favorite show or they might be with a friend they haven't seen. And the same goes when some parents come home and they are exhausted. They have no energy for the family thing. It doesn't mean they are not happy to see their family. They are just tired.

It is hard for any of us to be a light switch and suddenly turn "on." I also tell parents to give the kids transition time too. Parents try to wonder what these tough transitions mean and I think they just mean that none of us are light switches. It is nothing bigger than that.

—Richard

Children can react in several ways to a returning parent. Some children overwhelm you with attention and love. You may feel like you have a new appendage as your child clutches you, refusing to let go. Other children react differently. Sometimes they experience a jumble of emotions—part of them wants to hug their parent forever while another part of them is angry at being left behind. They approach you only to pull away. They may act disinterested in your return, or throw tantrums if you ask them to do something. If they are young, they may suddenly refuse to go to daycare or to have a babysitter.

You all need time to work it out together. Just as you are recovering from your trip, your family does a little recovering of their own. It's easy for you to plunge back into your chore routine, but your role as a parent might take a little more transition time. Here are some things you can do to help your whole family ease back to normal.

My four-year-old punishes his dad after he comes home. He usually won't talk to him on the phone and ignores him for an hour or so after he gets home. Then everything is fine. It breaks my husband's heart, but that is just how our little boy deals with his dad's absence.

—Jeannie

RETURNING HOME ACTIVITIES FOR YOU

- If possible, take a half day off from work to help you and your children reenter family life. Otherwise, it will appear to them that you are disappearing from their life again when you return to work.

- Encourage your children to bring out some of the memories they preserved during your trip. Schedule time to go over them together.

- Share journal entries you made during the trip that show how you missed your child.

- Make a cassette tape or write a note telling your child how much you love them and how much you missed them when you were away.

- Write "I'm so glad to be home!" on the message area of **Communication Central**.

- Help your child make an ongoing scrapbook of the photos, postcards and souvenirs that you bring home from each trip. You can talk briefly about each new item and where you collected it when you paste them in the album together.

- Invite each of your children on a personal outing tailor-made just for them—the ice cream parlor, a favorite park, and the video arcade are some suggestions.

- Thank the parent at home or the caregiver for a tough job well-done. If it is your partner, let them decide what their reward should be and schedule it during the first week back. If it is your caregiver, think of something thoughtful you could do for them.

- If you are married, make time for your partner. Make a date with them for dinner and/or a movie or an evening with just the two of you.

At some point you are balancing the parents' needs with the child's needs and parents need to get out of the house together. They need to step away from that parental role and focus on their relationship with each other at that point. That is a balancing act that we as adults need to figure out.

—Richard

7
MANAGING YOUR CHILD'S MEDICAL NEEDS

Doctor's visits can be incredibly stressful for kids. How many adults do you know who don't go to doctors? Nobody likes to be told that something is not working with them. Adults perform two functions when they accompany a child to the doctor: they translate any medical information into kid-friendly terms; and they ensure that any treatment the child receives is as free from physical or psychological trauma as possible.

—Richard

A sick child can really put a kink in a family schedule. For a time, everything is up in the air as you scramble to either take time off from work or find someone willing to be the stay-at-home nurse. Accidents bring the whole family's normal routine to a grinding halt. The phone call comes and you drop everything to rush to the hospital or doctor's office. You often arrive mid-treatment or, especially if you are out-of-town, after the treatment for the accident has already occurred. Health check-ups, dental appointments and ongoing medical treatments also force you to deviate from your customary routine.

As much as you want to be with your children for each and every medical crisis, sometimes you just can't. You can, however, make preparations ahead of time which will ease your stress level and reduce any trauma for your children. The best time to make clear-headed plans and decisions regarding the medical care of your children is now—in a nonemergency setting. Then, in the event a crisis occurs, you won't have to worry about medical permission slips or locating the right cold medicine. You can concentrate on what is most important—getting to your child and giving them your love and comfort.

PREPARING FOR AN ILLNESS AHEAD OF TIME

Even the onset of a bad cold can make the hardiest of us adults yearn for our mommies. Most working parents have felt more than a twinge of guilt when they had to leave a sick child. While you may not be there when your children get ill, you can lessen the guilt by being prepared ahead of time and knowing that they are well taken care of right from the first moment they feel bad.

ILLNESS SOOTHERS

- Make a **Comfort Kit** which can be pulled out whenever your child is feeling ill and can't attend school or daycare. Find a cardboard box or purchase a plastic container and fill it with the things you use when your child is ill. Some ideas for items to include in the **Comfort Kit** are:
  - Minor illness medications you use for colds, flu, fever and upset stomachs. Be sure to label each bottle with your child's name and specific directions.
  - A thermometer
  - Some of your child's comfort foods like pudding, a can of chicken noodle soup or a bottle of ginger ale
  - Art supplies or reading materials depending upon the age of your child. Some other suggestions are: coloring book and crayons; stickers and plain paper; colored construction paper, glue and scissors; books of mazes and dot-to-dots; favorite children's books or a comic book; a favorite video.
  - This kit can sit in a closet until it is needed. Give it to the person who is caring for your ill child and it can supply some comfort

until you can be with them. Don't forget to replace medications that go out-of-date and to restock items that have been used!

- Make copies of the **Get Well Checklist** on the next page and keep them in **Communication Central**. You can then give a copy to the person who will be taking care of your child or the adult at home can pull the form out when it is needed. It is a handy way to chart the progress of your child's illness and to note any medications he or she has received during your absence.

- Make copies of the **Authorization for Medical Care** on page 181. Be certain that your caregiver and anyone else who might attend to your child has a signed and witnessed copy. Also keep another original copy of the signed forms as well as blank authorizations in **Communication Central** just in case they are needed. Alert these caregivers to any allergic reactions your child has had to medications.

WHEN YOU RETURN HOME TO AN ILL CHILD

When you return home from work to a sick child, consider some of the following activities. They will make your child feel better, and you will feel good about giving your child some special attention. Sometimes it is hard with a busy family, but try to devote some time each evening exclusively to your sick child. If you end up taking a day off from work to care for your child, these activities will be a refreshing break for him or her from the usual TV and videos. They will also provide you and your child with some pleasant memories.

ACTIVITIES FOR PAMPERING YOUR ILL CHILD

- If their stomach is up to it, make or order in their favorite foods.

THE GET WELL CHECKLIST

Time that child first complained of feeling ill: _____

Symptoms:
- ❑ Runny nose   ❑ Green mucus   ❑ Clear mucus
  - ❑ Pain in _____
  - ❑ Cranky
  - ❑ Sore throat
  - ❑ Achy feeling
  - ❑ Rash or bumps
  - ❑ Fever :   _____ degrees at _____ am / pm
                 _____ degrees at _____ am / pm
                 _____ degrees at _____ am / pm
                 _____ degrees at _____ am / pm
  - ❑ Watery eyes
  - ❑ Cough
  - ❑ Tired
  - ❑ Vomiting

Medicine I've given: _____
   Last dose at: _____ am / pm

Did child respond to medicine?:
   ❑ yes How?_____
   ❑ no

Has child eaten?:
   ❑ yes What? _____
   ❑ no

Has child slept?:
   ❑ yes When? _____ am / pm
          How long? _____
   ❑ no

- If your child is not too ill to visit the store, or if you have a friend or neighbor willing to make the stop, check out travel videos from the store. The two of you can take a "vacation" by watching the videos together.

- Read to them, if you have time. Even older children enjoy being read to if it is the right book.

- Get them some new art supplies to get their creative juices flowing.

- Play one or two of their favorite card or board games. Or buy a new game and save it for a day when they are sick.

- Play any of the activities in the rest of this book.

- Tackle a long postponed task like sorting photos and putting them in an album—kids love to relive those memories along with you.

- Put on a slide show or drag out old home videos of your child.

- Make a "nest" of blankets, pillows, and stuffed animals in the living room. If it's winter, build a fire and "camp out" nearby.

- Get out something special for you and your child to play with: some possibilities are jewelry, a collection of any kind, old photo albums or yearbooks, make-up, your art supplies or small tools.

- Make paper dolls or fly paper airplanes.

- Deliver "room service" to your child. Give them a list of available "menu items" and pretend you are serving them in a hotel. Use a tray, cover the food with upside down bowls, and serve it with a flourish to them.

 Books for Young Children
Betsy and the Chicken Pox by Gunilla Wolde
Sick in Bed by Anne and Hartlow Rockwell
So Sick! by Harriet Ziefert
Farley Goes to the Doctor by Emily Kingsley

If You Have to Leave When Your Child Is Sick

If your child is sick for several days and you will either be out of town or cannot afford to take time off from work, don't despair. It's going to be hard on you not to be there, but you can nurse and parent your child from a distance by leaving things with the adult at home taking care of them.

Comforting Your Ill Child From a Distance

- Leave a Pampering List with the adult taking care of them. Write down any special care you want done for your child during the day. Ask them to mention that you arranged for the pampering hoping it would make your child feel better.

- Take out or create **The Comfort Kit** outlined on page 113.

- If your schedule permits it, call your child as often as possible to check up on how they are feeling. When you call them, ask them what is being done for them and what else they need. Be sure and communicate their needs to the adult taking care of them.

- If they get sick when you are away, tell them where a favorite tee shirt or night shirt of yours is and let them wear it while they are recuperating.

- Take an old tee shirt of yours and decorate it with fabric paints. Make it a **Get Well Shirt** that your sick child can wear while recuperating.

- Have the adult at home make ice cubes for your child out of a favorite juice or soda. Your child can suck on the ice cubes to soothe their scratchy throat.

- Leave some bubble bath, bath salts or a new bath toy so the adult at home can draw a great bath for your child.

- Ask the adult at home to teach your child a new card game.

- Buy—or check out from the library—books on cassette tapes for quiet listening time.

- Ask them to record their daily progress in their journals or on their cassette recorder. Give them a tape labeled **My Miserable Cold** or **My Days with the Flu.** Be sure to ask them to tell about the fun they are having as well as how they are recuperating.

- Read the chapter, **Building the Lines of Communication,** which starts on page 29. Some of these activities adapt beautifully to communicating with a sick child.

HANDLING ACCIDENTS BEFORE THEY HAPPEN

When any family member or friend experiences an accident, we use this as a learning opportunity for our children. We follow the healing process as a family. Then if our children ever experience a broken bone or a burn, we can remind them of how people they know and love have made it through their own trauma.

—Richard

If your child has a serious accident or develops a major illness, chances are that you will move mountains to be by his or her side when they are getting treatment. If you are on a business trip, you will finagle a seat on the first plane out of town even if you have to talk to the company president. There may come a time, however, when you are either out of the office or out of town, and can't be reached before your child needs medical treatment.

The most important thing you can do to plan for this is to make sure that the appropriate people have a medical permission slip for your child. This is doubly important if the other parent might be unavailable also. If you haven't done this already, copy the medical authorization form on page 181 and give it to anyone you think might ever need to use it— their teacher, the caregiver, a friends' parents and/or neighbors.

My boss, who is a doctor, and his wife, a nurse, were taking care of my two youngest children when my husband and I went to Mexico. My younger son got a 105° temperature and they had to take him to the emergency room. I had filled out the authorization for medical care before we left so everything was taken care of. We didn't even know about it until we got home. He couldn't have been in better hands.

—Heidi

AFTER THE ACCIDENT HAS OCCURRED

When there has been an accident or trauma, and you see your child for the first time, you want to try to find out what sort of state they are in. A child's affect is not always consistent with the way they are feeling. They could be laughing or making light of the whole situation and still be wounded.

—Richard

When you do reach your child, the first thing you will probably want to do is look them all over and see how they are with your own eyes. Then you will probably want to wrap them up in your arms and simply hold them. There will be time later to talk about the accident or the doctor's visit. For the first few moments, we all just want to make sure that our children are all right and that they know how very concerned we were and are. Talk to them and find out what they are feeling at that moment. If they are not crying, try to find out if they are currently traumatized by the accident or the trip to the doctor. Use the following techniques to troubleshoot their emotional health at the time of your return.

TECHNIQUES FOR TROUBLESHOOTING TRAUMA

- Ask your child to tell you all about the accident or the visit to the doctor. Use the worksheet called **My Accident** on page 121 as a guide for questions. You can go over this with your child or, if your child can read, copy it and they can fill it out on their own. Look for clues in their story or body language that will let you know if their experience was a traumatic one.

- For preschoolers, let them act out the treatment they received. For example, give them a play medical kit and let them pretend to give you stitches or put a cast on a part of your body. Watch to see how they play the doctor. This might give you some information about how they felt when they were treated. Be careful not to overinterpret their actions, though. They might simply be acting out their fear of what could have happened, not what actually happened to them.

- Ask your child to draw a picture of their experience, then have them describe what is happening in the drawing.

- Help them write and illustrate a story in their journal about their accident and their experience at the doctor's or the hospital.

- Observe their eating, sleeping and play habits for the next couple of days for any signs of lasting physical or psychological effects of the accident.

- Don't forget to be mindful of their reactions when they have either witnessed an accident or had a friend experience one. In either of those cases, they may experience some secondary trauma.

- If you do see signs of trauma, consult a mental health professional for the best way to treat it.

 Books for Young Children
Someday with My Father by Helen Buckley
Eric Needs Stitches by Barbara Davis Marino
Some Busy Hospital by Seymour Reit

MY ACCIDENT

What happened?: _____

_____

What I was doing when it happened: _____

_____

Where it happened: _____

_____

When it happened: _____

_____

Who I was with: _____

_____

How I felt: _____

_____

IF YOU WENT TO THE DOCTOR OR EMERGENCY ROOM:

What the doctor or nurse did: _____

_____

Tests they did:_____

_____

Did you have X-rays? Yes__ No__ How did they look?_____

_____

How much did it hurt?

No big deal!   Ouch!   It was bad!

Pain Thermometer

Medicine I need to take: _____

_____

Doctor's orders I need to follow: _____

_____

**On the back, draw a picture or write a story
about your accident.**

MISSING VISITS TO THE DOCTOR

Sometimes a conflict or a late breaking development at work makes it impossible for you to accompany your child to a medical appointment. This can or cannot present a problem depending upon how your child views a trip to the doctor. Even if you feel your child is usually unfazed by visits to the doctor, it's better to err on the side of making too much of the visit rather than minimizing its importance. In addition, your child's reaction to an office visit with the doctor may be quite different when accompanied by someone other than yourself. Prepare for the unexpected by using the following guidelines.

PREPARING YOUR CHILD FOR THEIR DOCTOR'S VISIT WITHOUT YOU

- Copy the **Check-up Checklist** on page 124 and the worksheet, **My Visit to the Doctor,** on page 125.

- Choose a time period close to the check-up to sit down with your child. Make sure it is a time when you both are relaxed and the house is somewhat quiet.

- Using the **Check-up Checklist** as your guide, explain exactly what is going to happen during their examination. If your child is young, you can use a play doctor's kit and go through the whole exam with you being the doctor first and then letting them have a turn at giving you a check-up.

- Ask them how they are feeling about going to the doctor. If this is a new doctor, tell your child anything you may know about the doctor— what the physician looks like, other children you know who have been to this doctor, and why you picked him or her.

- If they are nervous or afraid, remind them of other doctor's visits that have gone well. Talk about who is accompanying them to the doctor. Tell your child that you will tell the person going with them that they are a little nervous about the experience and need extra "tender loving care."

- Decide on a treat or reward for completing the doctor's visit. If they are going to get a shot, giving them a sugar cube to suck on just before their shot induces a calming effect.

- Give them a copy of **My Visit to the Doctor** and ask them to fill it out after the visit is over. If they are young, go over what they will do on the worksheet.

- Set a time to hear about the visit and go over the **My Visit to the Doctor** worksheet. If you are out of town, tell your child when you will call them to hear all about it and that you will look at the worksheet when you return.

Books for Young Children
The Check-Up by Helen Oxenbury
How the Doctor Knows You're Fine by Vicki Cobb
Come to the Doctor, Harry by Mary Chalmers
Going to the Doctor by Fred Rogers
Betsy and the Doctor and *Tommy Goes to the Doctor*
    by Gunilla Wolde

AFTER THE DOCTOR'S VISIT

Your child will have fun filling out the following worksheet after their visit to the doctor. If they are young, they will need help completing it from the adult that accompanies them. Copy this ahead of time and put it in a packet with a new box of crayons or markers, a sticker or two, or some sports cards. This is one more incentive to help your child sail through their exam. If your child is young, have the adult who accompanies the child encourage them to fill out as much of the worksheet as they can themselves.

When you get home, go over the worksheet with them. If they are young, play doctor again and let them show you their experience. Give them a chance to tell you their version of the check-up, then get out your mutually agreed upon reward for a check-up well-done.

CHECK-UP CHECKLIST

The nurse or doctor will probably:
❏ have them undress
❏ weigh your child
❏ find out how tall they are

Things the doctor might do:
❏ check their ears
❏ ask about what they eat
❏ check their throat
❏ feel their neck
❏ check their eyes
❏ look over their body
❏ take their blood pressure
❏ listen to their heart and lungs
❏ check their reflexes
❏ feel their abdomen
❏ ask them lots of questions

IMMUNIZATION SCHEDULE:

❏ DPT – 2 months, 4 months, 6 months, 18 months
❏ HIB – 2 months, 4 months, 6 months
❏ Polio – 2 months, 4 months, 18 months, 4-6 years
❏ DTap – 4-6 years
❏ Measles, Mumps, Rubella – 15 months, 5-18 years
❏ Tetanus – every ten years

MY VISIT TO THE DOCTOR

My name is: _____

I am _____ years old.

I am _____ ft. _____ inches tall.

I weigh _____ pounds.

My visit to the doctor today was: (check one)

❏ Real fun   ❏ Okay   ❏ Better than eating mushrooms   ❏ Yuck!

The best part of my visit was: _____
_____
_____

The worst part of my visit was: _____
_____
_____

Things the doctor said to me: _____
_____
_____

A drawing of my visit to the doctor
(in the space below or on the back):

MISSING SCHEDULED MEDICAL TREATMENTS

My son, Cory, is a severe asthmatic. He is on medications every day. We have trained his nanny to give him all the meds he takes. We also have a peak flow meter which she uses with him and charts the results. When he has an attack, she administers three or four medicines as he needs them and she charts them. She also has been trained to use his air pump delivery machine which atomizes his medicine. Cory has learned to become comfortable with any one of us treating him.

—Doug

If your child is undergoing regular medical treatments, chances are that you have developed a routine that you follow both before and after the treatment. If you have to be out of town during a treatment, you will have to talk to your child and let them be your guide as to how to handle your absence. Choose a time when both of you can concentrate on the issue at hand and use the suggestions below to help you make your child's treatment as trouble-free as possible.

PREPARING YOUR CHILD FOR YOUR ABSENCE FROM THEIR TREATMENT

- Ask them how they are feeling about going to their treatment without you.

- Query the child about who they would like to accompany them to their treatment. Do they want to "train" the substitute, or do they want you to prepare this caregiver?

- Explore whether they want to follow the same treatment routine or devise another one to follow whenever someone else takes them.

- Check to see if there is any place they would like to visit before their treatment. If it is OK for them to have some food, do they want to eat something special or stop at a particular restaurant before or after their treatment? Or would they rather go to a park before or after their appointment?

- Ask if they want the person taking them to go in with them when they receive the treatment.

- Investigate whether they want the person to hold their hand, read to them, or do anything else during the treatment.

- Give them something special of yours to hold or wear during their treatment.

PREPARING YOUR SUBSTITUTE FOR THE TREATMENT

No matter who your child picks to accompany them to their treatment—a loving aunt, a trusted adult friend or their long-time babysitter—the substitute will need to be prepared for all they might encounter. Here are some suggestions for prepping this person for the experience:

 ### BRIEFING YOUR STAND-IN

- Explain where to go, what time to arrive, and what, if anything, to bring.

- Explain the treatment itself. Tell them what it is, how it is administered, and how it feels. Tell them anything you know about it so that they will have empathy and understanding for your child.

- Tell them how your child usually acts before, during and after the treatment. Brief your substitute on any anxieties your child may have about their treatment.

- If your child wants to follow the usual treatment routine, explain it in detail. Tell them what you say and do when your child is upset.

- Arm your caregiver with any necessary props to take to the treatment such as favorite blankets, stuffed animals, good luck charms, or cassette tapes to be played in their Walkman during their treatment.

- Decide on a post-treatment treat or reward. Have your substitute tell your child it is from you and that you planned it especially for them.

- Leave a congratulations card for your child with the adult who will accompany them to treatment. Ask them to give it to your child immediately upon finishing treatment.

If you are out of town, call the night before the treatment and the night of the treatment to reinforce the fact that you know what is going on in your child's life and that you care about his or her reaction to the treatment. Tell your child that if they want to share the experience more with you to draw a picture, record their reactions on their cassette recorder, or write their feelings and thoughts in their journal. When you get home, be sure to make a date to sit down and go over everything they've written or done.

8
MISSING SPECIAL EVENTS, BIRTHDAYS AND HOLIDAYS

When you can't be there for an event or special day, a lot of fuss made beforehand can really help. Planning what they will wear, who will be attending, or dress rehearsing the big event—it's sure worked for me. Events, birthdays and holidays are really a big deal in my child's life and she wants some fuss made.
—Candi

With birthdays, plays, athletic tournaments and holidays, anticipation is as much a part of the excitement as the event or occasion itself. Each participant, parent and child alike, has their own vision of how the event or the special day will be played out. When the day finally arrives, these visions come together. Hopefully, expectations don't exceed reality and the event or special day is a success.

If you are going to miss such a special occasion, your absence may mean much more than a missing smile and hug. If you are the orchestrator of special activities for your family, then the occasion can assume quite a different tone without you. A key to making these special times successful when you can't be there is to help your family assess their expectations. Discuss what each member of the family envisions about the occasion, and whether or not these expectations might be realistic. Then use this chapter to help your child understand your absence and to add some celebratory activities of your own prior to the event or special day.

This chapter first examines missing events, such as a child's music recital or athletic game. If you will be missing a birthday or holiday celebration instead, look at the section later in this chapter, **Missing Out on Birthdays and Holidays**, starting on page 140.

—

HOW TO TELL YOUR CHILD YOU WILL MISS AN EVENT

You've just learned you won't be able to attend a special event your child has been anticipating, such as a dance recital or a sports tournament. One of the first things that has to be done is to personally inform your child. Express your regret sincerely and let your child know that you are disappointed about the turn of affairs. Don't assume they know how upset you are about not being able to be there. Take the time to show them that you are just as unhappy as they are about missing the event.

BREAKING THE NEWS TO YOUR CHILD

- Tell him or her personally in advance that you won't be able to attend the event. Explain the set of circumstances that will keep you away, and why you cannot change them. Tell the child how very sad and sorry you are. Explain that you know they are disappointed because you feel exactly the same way.

- Tell your child that you do not have a choice in this situation. Make it clear that it is your responsibility to attend this appointment, meeting, or class. Talk about your child's responsibility to attend school or participate in household chores. Explain to them that if there was a choice involved in this situation, you would choose to be with them.

- Talk to your child about their expectations for the big event before it actually happens.

- Ask for a "dress rehearsal" if you will be missing a performance. You may be able to view a practice or rehearsal for the actual event if you just ask. If that is not appropriate, ask your child to show you exactly what he or she will be doing. You could even set it up just like the real event—with costumes and all. This might be good practice for your child if they are nervous about performing at the actual event.

- Ask your child if they would like to invite anyone else to the event. If you have a partner who is able to attend, this alone may be enough. If you do not have a partner, think of someone else to invite. This person won't be a substitute for you, but rather someone who is available and able to make your child feel special on the big day.

- Tell your child how much you want to know everything that happens that day. Look over **Capturing the Event Itself** below and have your child help you determine the best approach. Next, make the necessary arrangements and let your child know you have taken those steps.

CAPTURING THE EVENT ITSELF

It was okay if I missed soccer practice, but my son would get very upset if I missed a soccer game. I was teaching on Thursday nights and sometimes a game would be scheduled for that night. When I got back from class, he and I would drag out the Playmobil figures and set them up on a pretend soccer field. Then he would move them around with a tinfoil soccer ball and give me a blow-by-blow narration of the game.

—*Pati*

After talking with your child about the event you will be missing, figure out how you are going to capture it. There are many ways. Some of the more common ones involve camcorders, cassette recorders and cameras. Taking the time to "capture" the event will go a lot further than simply telling your child how you wish you could be there. He or she will see arrangements being made and know how important their event is to you. After you return home and relive their important moments with them, you will have the feeling of knowing that you did your very best with a tough situation.

Everybody Say Cheese—Taking Photographs

Cameras have been capturing special events for over a hundred years. If the adult designated to accompany your child to the event is not handy with a camera, don't hesitate to ask someone else to document the event for you. They will be flattered at the compliment, and your child will have one more person there to make him or her feel special. If that is not possible, you can always ask other parents if you can have duplicates made of their pictures.

If you are the photographer in the family, don't assume that someone else can pick up your camera and use it like you do. You may have to give them a few lessons before the big day. Plan ahead and get all the kinks out of the system before the event occurs.

 ## Photo Tips

- Take before, during and after the event photos.

- If someone else is taking pictures for you, make sure they know how to use the equipment.

- Let the child in the event take some pictures if they are not too busy or distracted.

- The camera can be passed around to other friends and family members who are present for their photo perspective.

- Buy two or three disposable cameras. Hand them out to friends or family attending the event. Have them shoot the roll and return the cameras to you.

- Have two or three people document the event with their cameras.

- Hire a professional photographer to document the event for you.

Lights, Camera, Action— Recording an Event on Video

Camcorders have revolutionized your ability to preserve your child's special times. They are ideal for capturing a child's performance in a preschool "play" or an elementary school piano recital. If you don't own a camcorder, try to borrow one from a friend or look in your local yellow pages for a rental service store that carries them.

Video Basics

- Check your equipment ahead of time:
  - Is the battery charged?
  - Is there a blank tape?
  - Do you have the operation manual, just in case?
  - Will you need a tripod so that the person recording will be able to also watch and enjoy the event?

- If someone new is using your video camera, have a practice session.

- Record a dress rehearsal of the event.

- Record the pre-event preparations: dressing up, getting ready to go, arriving at the big event.

- Interview the participants before and after the event:
  - Are you excited, nervous, or cool and collected?
  - How did you think it went?
  - Would you want to do it again?
  - What was the most fun?

- If your child had friends participating in the event, interview them too.

- Interview friends and relatives about your child's performance. Then you'll have preserved the praise your child might not have heard on the big day.

- Hire a professional video group to make a tape of the event for you.

TESTING ONE, TWO, THREE— RECORDING ON AUDIO TAPE

Audio cassette recorders are often overlooked as a way to capture an event. The sounds they record can result in a lively documentation of the occasion. Tape recorders can also catch children during their most spontaneous moments. While children sometimes shy away from cameras, they seem to enjoy being silly when a microphone appears. Cassette recorders are especially good for pre- and post-event interviews.

MICROPHONE PLAY

- Tape record the actual event or a portion of it.

- Tape record your child's account of the event—what they wore, who was there, and what happened.

- Tape your child's feelings about the event—before and after. See the interview questions in **Lights, Camera, Action—Recording an Event on Video** on the previous page for ideas on what to ask.

- Pass the microphone around after the event to friends and relatives who attended. Have each of them give their account of your child's performance. Start with the child whose occasion it was and then let each friend or relative add to the story after the child is finished talking.

BRINGING OUT THE AUTHOR IN YOUR CHILD— WRITING ABOUT AN EVENT

Sitting down and writing about something gives your child a chance to reflect on what happened. If they enjoy keeping a journal, they might jump at the chance to put down their version of the event on paper.

THE WRITTEN WORD

- Ask your child to write an account of the event for you to read when you return. Some sample topics are:
  - How I felt before the event
  - The best part of the event
  - Our big moment—how the event actually went
  - How I wished the event had gone

- Suggest that your child make a story book about the event with illustrations. They can use either pictures they draw themselves or photos someone took at the event.

- Propose that your child make a comic book of what happened at the event.

- Ask your child to write a newspaper article about the event. What happened? Who was there? Supply them with a sample article from the newspaper to use as a guide.

THE BUDDING ARTIST—DRAWING A STORY BOARD

A story board is like a comic strip. The story is told or drawn in several different frames or panels. Young children can use this technique to capture a special occasion of theirs for you. Get them started with ideas for the drawings and, if they are young, have the adult at home write or record the child's description of each drawing panel. When you come home, sit down and ask the child to describe each picture to you. Ask them what is going on in specific parts of each picture.

PICTURE IDEAS FOR STORY BOARDS

- Getting Ready for the Event

- What I Wore

- Decorating for the Event

- Arriving at the Event

- My Part in the Event

- What Other Children Did

- Celebrating During or After the Event

- Coming Home

- Winding Down

———

NURTURING YOUR CHILD
ON THE DAY OF THE EVENT

It's important to make an effort to nurture your child on the actual day of the event. Here are some ideas that will give your child a boost when the big day finally arrives:

LONG-DISTANCE COMFORT

- Touch base the day of the big event with a phone call. If possible, talk before and after the event. You will be surprised how these two phone calls will keep you both connected.

- Arrange for your child to receive something special from you just before the important occasion. If you are out of town, you can either let the adult at home give it to them or you can give it to them before you leave. Some suggestions are: a new tie, belt, bow or piece of jewelry if the event requires dressing up; a book if it is an academic event; a treat or new piece of sports equipment for a sporting event; a certificate of accomplishment; flowers.

- If you made something with your child for the event, like a decoration or a special dish for a holiday, leave a reminder which tells them how much you enjoyed working on it with them. Be sure the adult at home knows the item is to be used that day.

HELP, I FEEL SO GUILTY!

If I have to be away from my children for a big event or holiday, I know that the day has the potential to be a distressing one. However, I try not to let it get the best of me, and I make sure that I treat myself well. I surround myself with friends if I can, or treat myself to something I know will make me feel better—a good workout, a phone call to my kids, or work I particularly enjoy.
—Pati

The big day can be difficult to live through. Sometimes the guilt just gets the best of you. Instead of concentrating on what you are *not* doing as a parent, think about all that you *are* doing as a parent, person and employee.

RELIEVING YOUR GUILT

- If you are out of town, treat yourself to something special the night of the event: dinner out, a movie or play—something that will provide a little distraction.

- If you are working, be proud of what you are accomplishing at work, instead of dwelling on what you are missing at home.

- Think of all the benefits your job brings to your family.

- Remember that you are not the only parent who has ever missed a special event in their children's lives.

- Remember how resilient children are. Yes, your child might be mad at you for missing this occasion, but they will get over it.

- Think of the good things you have done for your child lately. This event is not the only opportunity for you to be a good parent. Your parenting skills are not measured by your attendance at this event.

- Remind yourself that you have made every attempt to "capture" the event and plan a special celebration of your own with your child. *You have done the best you can.*

RETURNING HOME AFTER THE BIG EVENT

We have video taped some events for Kit when he was gone. We loved to watch the tapes over and over, and when Kit would come home, we would watch them as a family. The child in the event gets to give the play-by-play and the rest of us get to chime in when we had something to add. Sometimes watching the video is as much or more fun than the actual event!
—Heidi

You never know what you will encounter when you get back home after missing an important occasion. Your child might bombard you with details. They might be angry about your absence and ignore your questions. Or the event may have already faded into a distant memory. Make every attempt to let your child share as much of the event with you as they want. All the preparations in the world before the event can be undermined by too little attention afterwards.

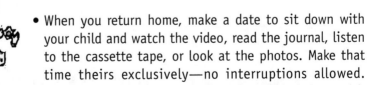

TIPS FOR RELIVING THE EVENT WITH YOUR CHILD

- When you return home, make a date to sit down with your child and watch the video, read the journal, listen to the cassette tape, or look at the photos. Make that time theirs exclusively—no interruptions allowed. However, don't push. If your child is angry, they may try to punish you for not being there. Apologize again for missing the event and give them a chance to cool off before you try to set a time for talking about the event.

- Ask your child to tell you all about the event. Let your child's enthusiasm determine how far to take the event replay. You can interview them and record it.

- Ask your child to act out what actually happened at the event.

- If you were unable to attend an athletic event, ask your child to show you "key" plays that occurred during the game. Set up army men, or use Legos as the players in the game. Have your child move them around demonstrating how a score or a specific play was made.

- Encourage the budding director in your child by having them design a play patterned after the big occasion. You and the family or their friends can be the actors while they direct you.

- Turn the replay into an event itself—offer popcorn, milk shakes or a special treat to be enjoyed while you talk about the big occasion.

- Make a photo album of pictures taken at the event with your child.

- Convey how you hated to miss the event. Tell them that you are glad they had their big day, but that you were very sad to miss it. If there is an event on the schedule that you will be able to make, let them know now. If you can make changes to your schedule so that you will be able to catch these events from now on, tell them the good news.

- Make a date with your child—a time for just the two of you. A special date will help reassure your child how important he is to you.

If your child is not interested in viewing the video or discussing the occasion with you, don't feel deflated. Look at the up side! Your child knows you made every effort to compensate for your absence. You have preserved moments which you can now watch, read or hear and make part of your memories. Think twice before you assume that your efforts were wasted. If another scheduling conflict arises, try again. Next time, the results may be very different.

MISSING OUT ON BIRTHDAYS AND HOLIDAYS

Missing out on a birthday or a holiday can be a little different than missing a big event. Family routines and holiday rituals cannot be as easily "captured" as a piano recital or a hockey game. Instead of everything happening in a one- or two-hour window, birthday and holiday celebrations can last the whole day—longer if friends and family are visiting from out of town. If you are going to be away for a birthday or holiday that is important to your family, consider having some type of celebration of your own before you leave. It doesn't have to be like the one you usually have—sometimes a new twist on celebrating a holiday can be just as memorable as the big event itself.

This section includes suggestions for missing a birthday and many of the major holidays. Each page has lots of activities that you and your children can do before or after the actual day. Pick an activity or two for the holiday you will miss, and your child's memories will be expanded—not ruined.

Since it was impractical to include all the holidays celebrated in this country, those that are the most commonly celebrated have been included here. If a holiday that is important in your household is not listed, use **Advance Activities for Birthdays or Any Holiday** on the next page to help you get started. There might also be activities for particular holidays that can be adapted to other holidays as well.

Something we have started in our family is to try to teach our children to take a look around them at the world outside our front doors. Around holiday time, we ask them to see if there is someone in the neighborhood that could use some help—raking leaves, shoveling snow, or carrying packages. That gives them a sense of noticing who in their own little world could use some help.
—Heidi

ADVANCE ACTIVITIES FOR BIRTHDAYS OR ANY HOLIDAY

- Arrange to have your birthday or holiday celebration before you have to leave. If your family wants, they can also have a small celebration the actual day. Moving up the celebration can seem strange to adults, but children rarely mind.

- Make a centerpiece or room decoration with your child using the birthday or holiday theme. They can bring this out on the big day.

- Decorate your home with your children in the birthday or holiday theme.

- Buy a lapel pin, earrings or socks with the birthday or holiday theme for yourself and your child. Both of you can wear them on the big day. When you call to wish them a happy birthday or holiday, you can tell your child you are wearing the item.

- Cook a favorite food together that you both love. This item can be served at the celebration.

- Take a piece of colored posterboard and write or draw a birthday or holiday greeting on it. Now cut it up into jigsaw-shaped pieces for a custom-made puzzle. If your children are young, make the pieces large. If they are older, cut lots of pieces for a real challenge. Have the adult at home give it to them on the big day.

- Take a trip to the library and check out books that are written around the birthday or holiday theme. You can select several and read one or two a day up to the time you have to leave.

- Call a homeless shelter, nursing home or other agency that helps needy people and ask them how you and your children might help make the holiday brighter for their residents.

- Make a mural of what the birthday or holiday means to your family. Buy butcher paper and tear off an appropriate length piece. Each night, you and your children can add a little bit to the mural as part of your bedtime routine. Hang it up for a truly personal and unique birthday or holiday decoration the day you have to leave.

- Make a banner or flag with your child and fly it in a window of your home before and on the holiday.

- Ask your child what they think is the perfect way to spend the birthday or holiday. If it is possible or practical, execute their plan on a day you will be there.

 Books for Young Children
The Family's Read Aloud Holiday Treasury by Alice Low
Ring Out, Wild Bells: Poems About Holidays and Seasons
    by Lee Bennett Hopkins
The Children's Book of Jewish Holidays and *A Picture Book*
    of Jewish Holidays by David Adler
Celebrations by Myra Cohn Livingston

BIRTHDAY AND HOLIDAY CELEBRATIONS

Birthdays

Birthdays are celebrated differently in homes across the country. If birthdays are a big deal in your home, and you won't be there on the actual birthday, make sure to make an extra fuss over your child before the big day.

Birthday parties are rarely held on a child's actual birth date. Up until children develop the ability to use a calendar, they do not even know what day their birthday falls on. Try to make every attempt to schedule your child's birthday party or celebration on a day when you can be there.

If a crisis crops up at work after the invitations have been sent and the plans for the festivities have already been made, try two things: capture the party using some of the techniques in **Capturing the Event Itself** starting on page 131 and also try one or two of these pre-birthday activities.

BIRTHDAY ACTIVITIES

- Have a birthday dinner for the family and a special friend of the birthday child. Let the birthday child pick out the menu from start to finish.

- Make cupcakes with your child to share with their daycare or school friends as a birthday snack.

- Make an audio or video tape telling your child all about the day they were born or the day you first saw your child if he or she is adopted. Add to the production each year, describing some of the milestones your child has experienced during the past year.

- Make a tape about your child's milestones from their point of view. Interview them about what has happened in the past year. Save it and add to it every year. They will have a great time listening to it, now and when they are grown.

- Make sure that you still arrange something (a special dinner perhaps) in recognition of the actual day. Leave a card at home for them or send them something via express delivery service.

- If you want to leave a present at home for them, why not design a treasure hunt? You can prepare clues ahead of time and leave them with the parent or caregiver. You can also fax or e-mail the clues to them.

- Take some time to sit down and talk about all the events and milestones they have reached during the past year. Write them down and start keeping a birthday book.

 Books for Young Children
Pancake Pie by Sven Nordquist
Won't Somebody Play With Me? by Steven Kellogg
Happy Birthday to Me by Anne and Harlow Rockwell
On the Day You Were Born by Debra Frasier
Happy Birth Day by Robie Harris

Valentine's Day

Valentine's Day is actually the combination of two very old celebrations. In 496 A.D., the Pope designated February 14 as the feast day of Saint Valentine, a priest who gave aid to persecuted Christians. February 15 is the old Roman holiday of Lupercalia—a lovers' festival where each boy found his partner by drawing her name from a box. Somehow the two celebrations have become intertwined and Valentine's Day on February 14 has become our day to declare our affections for others.

Valentine's Day is the perfect day to send a special love message to your children. Make your valentine ahead of time, then either have the adult at home give it to them or hide it yourself and give them clues over the phone regarding its location. Or try some of the other activities that you and your child can do together before you leave.

VALENTINE'S DAY ACTIVITIES

- Buy a large piece of poster board and write a **Candy Bar Valentine** greeting on it. Wherever the words appear in capital letters, paste the candy bar with that name in the space instead of writing the word. Here is an example:

- The day you were born was the best **(PAYDAY)** of my life. You will always be special to me—both **(NOW AND LATER)**. Even when you are a **(SMARTIE)** or have **(BUTTERFINGERS)**, I am lucky to have you. Most of the time, you make me feel like a **(MILLIONAIRE)**. I love you more than all the stars in the **(MILKY WAY)**.

- Make a valentine on a piece of colored construction paper with a message composed of simple words and pictures cut out from magazines. This is especially good for beginning readers.
  - Here's a sample message. Cut out a picture or make a drawing for the bolded words in parentheses: You are the **(apple)** of my **(eye)**. I love you!

- Make a "book" for your child called **10 Things I Love About You**. Take six sheets of plain paper and fold them in half. Staple them along the fold and you have a book! Decorate the cover and write the numbers 1-10 in large letters on each page. Then, under each number, write a reason you love your child.

- Help your child make valentines for his or her classmates or daycare playmates.

- Make heart-shaped cookies and decorate them together with icing. The no-fuss way to do this is to buy prepared sugar cookie dough, roll it out, and cut the shapes with a cookie cutter. Decorate them with the tubes of squeeze icing you can buy ready-made.

Books for Young Children
One Zillion Valentines by Frank Modell
Miss Flora McFlimsey's Valentine by Mariana
The Best Valentine in the World by Marjorie Weinman Sharmat
Love Notes by Kate Buckley
Things to Make and Do for Valentine's Day by Tomie De Paola

Easter

In your family, Easter may be a joyous religious holiday celebrating Christ's rising from the dead, a chance for the Easter Bunny to pay a visit to your children, or both. Some families dress up in new spring outfits for their church services or for a special meal with friends and family. Pick pre-Easter activities that reflect this holiday's role in your home.

If You Celebrate Easter as a Religious Holiday

- Tell the story of Easter one night before bed.

- Ask your child to tape or sing one of the songs from the Easter service to help you share in the event.

- Dress up in your Easter Sunday finery and take pictures of the family. Since you won't be there on the big day, plan an excursion you all can take to show off your outfits.

- On each special day in Lent—Palm Sunday, Maundy Thursday and Good Friday—sit your children down and talk about what happened on that day. This is one of the best ways to make them realize that the Easter story encompasses a long period—not just one day.

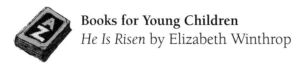

Books for Young Children
He Is Risen by Elizabeth Winthrop

IF A VISIT FROM THE EASTER BUNNY IS A PART OF YOUR HOLIDAY

- Tell your children that the Easter egg symbolizes birth and a "new beginning." Explain that the ancient Egyptians thought that Earth had hatched from a giant egg.

- Decorate eggs together. Let your child color a paper cutout of an egg you can take to work with you.

- Stage an egg hunt before or after you come home.

- Have your children hide eggs for you. They'll love watching you search high and low.

- Make Easter bonnets by making or buying old hats at the thrift store and have an "Easter Parade" around the house or neighborhood.

- Balance a decorated hard-boiled egg on a spoon and have a race around the room with your children. If you have lots of people, have a relay race.

Books for Young Children
Easter Parade by Mary Chalmers
The Bunny Who Found Easter by Charlotte Zolotow
The Easter Bunny that Overslept by Priscilla Freidrich
The Adventures of Egbert the Easter Egg
    by Richard Willard Armour

Passover

Passover is the Festival of Freedom for Jewish people. It is a time when they commemorate the Hebrews leaving Egypt after over four hundred years of slavery to the Pharaohs. It is also a time to celebrate the coming of spring. Passover is celebrated with family and friends coming together at a Seder—it's a time for eating special foods, saying prayers and singing songs.

PASSOVER ACTIVITIES

- Talk about the four questions. When you are discussing "Why is this night different from all the others," explain that your absence will be one more difference that night.

- Sit your children down and talk about the foods eaten at the Seder. Explain the significance of each of these items.

- Tell them the story of Passover one night before they go to bed. Have your whole family act it out.

- Tell your children about the origin of matzo—how the Hebrews had to flee in such a hurry that their bread did not have time to rise. Make matzo balls together.

- Check out some children's books dealing with Passover from the library and read them together.

- Talk about the differences and similarities in the Seder you will attend and the one your child will be attending.

- Before you leave, invite some non-Jewish friends over to hear the story of Passover. It could be a chance for a great cultural exchange.

- Help your child prepare an activity for their school or daycare to explain your family's traditions for Passover. Go to their school or daycare with them and help them explain why they will be eating certain foods for the coming week.

- Teach your child to make Charoses. Keep it until the Seder and have your child share it with the others.

- Discuss the phrase used at the Seder, "Let all who are hungry come and eat." Explain how someone will be welcoming you and/or your family to their table during your absence.

Books for Young Children

The Four Questions by Lynne Sharon Schwartz
The Carp in the Bathtub by Barbara Cohen
The Magician by Uri Shulevitz
Matzoh Mouse by Lauren Wohl
A Picture Book of Passover by David Adler
Happy Passover, Rosie by Jane Breskin Zalben

Fourth of July

Independence Day makes us think of fireworks, picnics and summer fun. This day commemorates the birth of our country—the day the Declaration of Independence was signed. Our celebrations are really birthday parties for our country. You can't reschedule the big city fireworks show, but other ways we celebrate this holiday are all easily done in advance.

FOURTH OF JULY ACTIVITIES

- Make flags and have a parade around the house or neighborhood. Bring along a red wagon, trikes and bicycles. Add streamers to the handlebars.

- Tell your children about the Declaration of Independence. Write a declaration for your family and have each child give it their "John Hancock"—just like the signers of the Declaration of Independence. If you can find a feather, try sharpening it, dipping it in ink and signing the declaration the way our forefathers did.

- Light a candle outside and see who can put it out first with a water pistol.

- If it is legal in your area, have a fireworks display of your own. Vote for the best fireworks.

- Make a birthday cake for the United States. Have the kids decorate it with squeeze-type tubes of red, white and blue icing. Put sparklers in it for candles and light them. The children can take turns waving sparklers and "writing" things in the air.

- Sing the national anthem, "The Star Spangled Banner." Also sing "America the Beautiful." Ask your children which one they would vote for as our national anthem. If they don't know the songs already, ask them if they would like to learn them.

- Read some of the Declaration of Independence. Explain to your children that Thomas Jefferson wrote it to escape the tyranny of King George III—in spite of being threatened with death. Ask your children what "causes" they feel are worth standing up for.

 Books for Young Children
The Fourth of July Story by Alice Dalgliesh
Fourth of July by Barbara M. Joosse
Henry's Fourth of July by Holly Keller
Hooray for the Fourth of July by Wendy Watson
Fourth of July Bear by Kathryn Lasky

Rosh Hashanah and Yom Kippur

Rosh Hashanah celebrates the beginning of the Jewish New Year. It begins the observance of the Ten Penitential Days—the most solemn period of the Jewish year. This whole period is a time for reflection on one's personal behavior during the past year and it culminates when Yom Kippur, the most sacred of Jewish holidays, is observed. Yom Kippur is a day of confession, repentance and prayers for the forgiveness of sins committed during the year. Both of these holidays are known as the High Holy Days.

ROSH HASHANAH

- Dip apples in honey and talk about the tradition of using this food to wish everyone a sweet year. Remind your child that on the holiday itself you will be thinking about this time that you spent together.

- Make honey cake or buy it from a bakery the night before you leave. Have your child present it to the family gathered for the holiday.

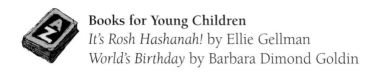

Books for Young Children
It's Rosh Hashanah! by Ellie Gellman
World's Birthday by Barbara Dimond Goldin

Yom Kippur

- Before you leave, help your child examine his or her life for the past year. Make lists of things they have done well and areas they would like to improve. Be sure to include some examples from your own life to help them get going. They will have their list ready and waiting for Yom Kippur.

- In advance of the holiday, sit down with your children and talk about things others have done to them during the past year. Talk about the concept of forgiveness and help them think of ways they can forgive and put the incidents behind them. You can also discuss ways of making amends to someone who has been wronged. When you call them on Yom Kippur, ask them to share any further thoughts they have had about these concepts.

- In the days of the Temple of Jerusalem, the high priest would place his hands on a goat as he confessed the people's sins. The goat was then taken to the wilderness and thrown over a precipice. The sacrificial act was symbolic of God's forgiveness. The concept of the scapegoat actually originated in this ancient ceremony. Tell your children about the origination of the word and how it means "someone who bears the blame for others." Talk with your children about how the word is used today.

Books for Young Children
Minnie's Yom Kippur Birthday by Marilyn Singer

Halloween

Dressing up in costumes is popular any time of the year. Halloween—celebrated on October 31—is especially fun because everybody can get into the act. Halloween started in ancient Britain when the Druids dressed up in frightening costumes to scare away winter's evil spirits. Now All Hallows Evening has become a night of merrymaking that can be easily celebrated before the actual event.

HALLOWEEN ACTIVITIES

- Have your children dress up in their Halloween costumes in advance and arrange for them to go trick-or-treating at a neighbor's or friend's house. It makes it more fun if you dress up too.

- Carve a Jack-o-lantern together. Carve one with each child if you have the time and energy. If you don't have time to carve a pumpkin, paint on a face or stick on vegetables for the features with toothpicks: cherry tomatoes for eyes, a carrot for a nose, a squash for a mouth and gourds for ears.

- If your child has a school carnival, volunteer to help in the preparations before the event. You can share what's going on with your child.

- Get together with your child and make a trick-or-treat bag. Get a paper bag and decorate it with markers, crepe paper and/or cutouts. This way they will take a bit of you trick-or-treating with them on Halloween night.

- Turn paper plates into scary masks one evening. Cut out eyes, a nose, and a mouth, then decorate it with markers, yarn or cloth scraps. Punch holes in the sides and tie on ribbon or yarn to hold it on.

Books for Young Children

The Vanishing Pumpkin by Tony Johnston

The Dragon Halloween Party by Loreen Leedy

Halloween Surprises by Ann Schweninger

Halloween by Gail Gibbons

Witches, Pumpkins and Grinning Ghosts: The Story of Halloween Symbols by Edna Barth

Thanksgiving

Thanksgiving—celebrated on the fourth Thursday in November—makes most of us think of friends, family and food—the smell of a turkey roasting and pies baking. The turkey is not the only one that gets stuffed, though. We sit around our tables eating probably the biggest dinner of the year.

The first Thanksgiving was very much like that. The Pilgrims were celebrating an abundant harvest, and they wanted to thank the Indians for sharing their knowledge about their land and food. It was a feast and a time of sharing for all of them. We carry on the tradition by sharing our food with others and reflecting upon our own blessings.

THANKSGIVING ACTIVITIES

- Sit down with your family one night and make a list of all the things your family is thankful for. Take turns suggesting items for the list. Decorate it and hang it in the message area of **Communication Central** for everyone to see.

- Get together with your children and imagine how the Pilgrims felt coming to a new land. Ask your children what they would do for food, clothing and toys if you and your family suddenly relocated to the woods and lived in a tent.

- Reverse the roles and now imagine how the Indians felt when strange people moved into their home. Ask your children if there have been any new kids at their daycare or school. How have they been treated? Is there anyone they know now that could use a helping hand?

- If you know of someone new in your neighborhood or school, ask them over for a **Welcome and Sharing Dinner**.

- Find out what group in town is requesting turkeys for the homeless. Take the kids to the grocery store with you and purchase the turkey. Include them also when you deliver it. Explain to them the many ways you can extend "Thanksgiving" into the community.

- Some groups in town solicit "cooked" Thanksgiving dinners. If you have the time, you can prepare ahead of time everything except the turkey. You can make pies or veggie casseroles with your children. The morning of Thanksgiving, your family can make the deliveries and remember the fun they had with you making the food. The spirit of giving will never be so graphic.

Books for Young Children

One Terrific Thanksgiving by Marjorie Sharmat
Don't Eat Too Much Turkey by Miriam Cohen
The Feast of Thanksgiving by June Behrens
How Many Days to America? by Eve Bunting
Thanksgiving at the Tappletons by Eileen Spinelli

Chanukah

Chanukah is also known as the Festival of Lights. Each night a candle on the menorah is lit until all eight candles are burning. This candle lighting commemorates the time the Hebrews recaptured their Temple of Jerusalem from the Syrians and found their "eternal light" extinguished. When they rededicated the temple, they found that there was only enough lamp oil for one day's worth of light. However, when it was lit, it burned until more oil was brought—a period of eight days. The small band of Hebrews was thus successful in defending their temple.

Chanukah is celebrated now with games and a gift exchange on each of the eight nights of the holiday. If you have to be gone for some or all of Chanukah, try a few of these activities before you go.

CHANUKAH ACTIVITIES

• Make or buy a menorah with your child for their room. Make menorahs and Jewish stars with colored construction paper to hang on the walls for decorations throughout the holidays.

• Act out the story of Chanukah.

- Make a dreidel out of a pencil and small square cardboard box.

- Ask your children why they think that the lamp burned for so long on such a small amount of oil. Ask them to tell you about things they have seen that are amazing. Talk about what gives people strength to overcome huge odds. Join in with a few stories of your own.

- Prepare ahead of time for the days of Chanukah you will miss. Leave little gifts with the parent or caregiver at home.

- Phone, e-mail or fax your home each day of Chanukah—around the time when the candles are being lit, if possible.

- Start writing a Chanukah story with your children before you leave. Throughout the days you will be gone, add to this story daily and fax or e-mail your addition to them. Or maybe you and your children can take turns adding to the story. Upon your return, you can "self-publish" the story and have a new family treasure.

- Talk with your children about who is not free in our current world and who is fighting for their religious freedom.

- Teach your children to make latkes, or make them for the holiday and freeze them ahead of time.

 Books for Young Children
It's Chanukah! by Ellie Gellman
Laughing Latkes by M. B. Goffstein
Beni's First Chanukah by Jane Breskin Zalben
A Picture Book of Hanukkah by David Adler
Just Enough Is Plenty by Barbara Dimond Golden
The Spotted Pony by Eric Kimmel

Christmas

In the Christian church, Christmas is the annual celebration of the birth of Christ held on December 25. In our culture, it is much more than one day. It is a season kicked off by the media as soon as the Thanksgiving dinner dishes are cleared. It is a fast-paced, exciting four weeks of shopping, parties, visits to Santa, anticipation, housecleaning and decorating. In some houses, Christmas Eve is the time for the actual Christmas celebration. Other families celebrate on Christmas day, opening presents in the morning and enjoying an afternoon dinner. Unless you are going to be away for an extended period of time, you will still be able to savor much of Christmas.

CHRISTMAS ACTIVITIES

- Set up a Nativity scene in your home. For several nights, tell the story of Christmas using the figurines in the scene as "actors." Let your children move them around as you tell the story. Pretty soon, they will be able to tell the story too.

- Make or buy an ornament. Paint your name on it or paste your picture to it. Tell your children you will be with them on their tree. You can also do this for loved ones who cannot be with you because of geography or because they have died.

- Make a wish ladder. Take two long pieces of string and cut out twenty-five pieces of colored construction paper. Each day of December ask your child what they are thankful for and write it on one rung of the ladder (the colored piece of construction paper) and attach it to the string. Each child can make a wish ladder.

- Pick a tree outside and decorate it with popcorn and cranberry strings for the birds and colored lights for you and your children. Whenever your children see birds on the tree or the lights at night, they will think of the fun you all had decorating it.

- Pick a name off of an angel tree or get the name of a needy child from your church or school. It is especially meaningful if the youngster is the same age and sex as your child. Then plan a shopping trip with your child to buy a present. Give him or her a budget and let the child pick the present out. Celebrate the sharing spirit afterwards with hot chocolate.

- Take your child to see *A Christmas Carol* or an age-appropriate Christmas play or pageant.

- Make Christmas cookies or candy with your children and deliver them to friends together.

- Make or buy sweet rolls for your family to have on Christmas morning.

- Pick up a holiday craft magazine and make one or more of the ornaments with your children. Personalize them with your child's name for an extra special touch. Whenever your child sees them, they will think of you.

- Take your child to shop for presents for the other important people in their lives.

- Watch the movies *Miracle on 34th Street* or *It's a Wonderful Life* as a family.

IF YOU WILL MISS BOTH CHRISTMAS EVE AND CHRISTMAS DAY

- Plan ahead. Make sure you have left presents or remembrances at home under the tree for your family.

- Ask your family to put together some Christmas goodies for you to take with you in your suitcase.

- Plan a special holiday dinner before or after your trip

- Ask a family member to video tape the kids opening the presents.

- Don't set yourself up for disappointment. Holiday telephone lines are very busy. Pick a realistic time to get through to your family or agree to talk after Christmas Day.

- Reach out wherever you are for the holidays. If you end up someplace unexpectedly, ask yourself if there is a family friend, relative or an acquaintance that you could join. Even if it means renting a car, it may be worth it to be with another family or a friend on this day.

- If you are alone, find out if there is a holiday performance or church service which may help to make the day special for you.

Books for Young Children
There are so many Christmas books to share and each family has its favorites. One that does deal with separations at Christmas is *Grandpa and Bo* by Kevin Henkes.

Kwanzaa

Kwanzaa is the African American festival of the harvest. It begins on December 26 and lasts for seven days. The word Kwanzaa comes from the Kiswahili language and means "first fruits." The celebration was created in 1966 by an African American named Maulana Karenga as a way to restore African cultural traditions to the African American people.

KWANZAA ACTIVITIES

- In advance of your absence, sit down with your children and talk about the particular day or days of Kwanzaa you will miss most. Discuss the principles of Kwanzaa which apply to those particular days.

- If possible, call home on the days of Kwanzaa and discuss the principle of the day and how it applies to your life and those of your children.

- Help your children make the Kwanzaa symbols before you leave or upon your return.

- On each day that you are gone, fax or e-mail a hand drawing of the appropriate Kwanzaa symbol. Ask your children to draw one for you also.

- If you will be gone for all or most of Kwanzaa, give your children a thin, blank notebook. Ask them to make a Kwanzaa book. They can write the principles and draw and color the symbols. They can also write about what their African heritage means to them and draw the continent of Africa. Preschoolers can cut out appropriate pictures from magazines and paste them in the book. The adult at home can write down captions for their pictures which you can read with them upon your return.

- If you will be missing the Kwanzaa Karamu (feast on the last day of Kwanzaa), talk with your family about meal preparations before you leave. Maybe you can prepare a dish with your children and freeze it. If there will be readings by family members, prepare your reading and give it to someone to read for you on the day of the feast.

- Purchase a tape or CD of Kwanzaa music or music played with African instruments. Give it to your family upon your departure.

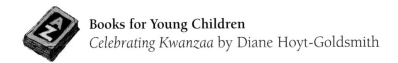

Books for Young Children
Celebrating Kwanzaa by Diane Hoyt-Goldsmith

REFLECTING ON MISSED HOLIDAYS AND SPECIAL EVENTS

Surviving a birthday or holiday without your family is a challenge, but like all of life's challenges, it also holds its moments of sweetness. Poignant telephone conversations on the special day, listening to your children excitedly tell you about the event when you return home, and the realization that your absence did not ruin the day for your child—all of these elicit feelings of thankfulness for a crisis successfully averted. Along with that is the promise of gratitude when future special occasions arise and your family's celebration is held with all of its members gathered together.

9
HARNESSING
YOUR EMOTIONS

When I leave for work, my little girl is still snuggled in her bed sound asleep. When I come home, we only have two and a half hours before she has to go to bed. I constantly fear that I just am not spending enough time with her.
—Rose

All of us at one time or another have probably shared these feelings of guilt and fear for our children. A small dose can be very healthy. Fears about our children's safety prompt us to question if our children are in a safe and loving environment. However, sometimes these feelings can take on a life of their own. They can loom larger than life in our minds and result in sleepless nights. If they are getting the best of you, it may be time to consult with a counselor. However, it is often possible to tame these emotions and channel them into more positive activity.

EVALUATING YOUR EMOTIONS

Having my kids in daycare was my biggest guilt. I would have given any-thing to have something to help me through that. There were days when they would scream, "I don't want to go, I don't want to go!" And then there were days when they would scream "I don't want to go home!" I felt guilty the whole time. I felt guilty for taking them and I felt guilty for picking them up.

—Mary

Sometimes our personal baggage or an emotionally charged situation makes it difficult to assess our feelings. Use the techniques below to help you evaluate exactly what it is you are feeling.

A PROCESS FOR WORKING THROUGH YOUR FEELINGS

1. Identify the emotion and its cause.
- Is it fear about your children's safety?
- Are you feeling guilty about the limits on the amount of time you can spend with them?
- Is your child having a problem you are worried about?
- Do you have nagging feelings about the person who takes care of your children?

Your feeling: I feel _____ because _____.

Example: By the time I return from work at the end of the day, it is 6 pm. I cook dinner, clean up and help out with homework. Then it is time for baths and bedtime. I constantly feel as though I have no quality time with my kids.

I feel <u>sad and guilty</u> because <u>I do not have enough time with my children</u>.

2. What triggered it?
- When did you first notice this feeling, or when did it first start really bothering you?

Example:
- It is an ongoing feeling I have had for some time.
- I recently started to feel that I always get the dirty work—prodding the children to do homework, take a bath, get dressed for bed—it seems there is no time for fun.

- Now that my kids are older, I have a feeling of sadness that I am missing out on my children's lives.

3. Evaluate the problem.
- Is this problem a safety issue? If the answer is yes, you must address it right away. Investigate the situation as soon as you possibly can and act on what you find. Find out if your fears are correct. If they are, you have to make some changes.
- Is this problem out of your control? If the answer is yes, read through the section **Accepting What You Can't Control** starting on the next page.
- Is this problem within your control? Ask yourself the following:
  —Do my children perceive this to be a problem also?
  —Is this problem temporary? Will it self-correct within a short time?
  —If this problem is of a more permanent nature, am I willing to make any changes?
- In simple terms, state the problem.

Example: You've taken a look at your appointment book and you realize that you are not spending much time with your children. You find that they also feel they are not getting enough of your time. They say they do not get enough one-on-one time with you. This situation is not temporary.

Problem: My children need more time with me.

4. Make a list of potential solutions.

Example:
- Sit down with your child and brainstorm possible solutions.
- Explore ways to free up some of your time. Look at your appointment book again. Is there work time that is not spent efficiently? Can you take a lunch hour one day a week and eat this meal with your child? Can you afford any help with your household work? Can you eliminate any activities from your schedule?
- Make a special weekly date with each of your children.
- Participate in an ongoing activity with your children.

5. Prioritize the solutions.
- Look over your potential solutions and decide what is doable and what is a pipe dream. Explain the reasons something is not practical to your children.

6. Take action.
- Plan to put your number one solution into place as soon as you can.

After taking stock of your feelings, and identifying solutions, take some action. Prioritizing your solutions is an important step. What will work for you and your family? Don't assume that because something works for a co-worker, it will be suitable for you. When you do decide on a plan of action, include your child in some of the decisions about how to implement it, if that is appropriate. Take it slowly. Unless the problem has to do with your child's safety, you don't have to solve the problem immediately. If you take time to work it out, you can analyze how it is going each step of the way and make necessary adjustments in your approach.

My children walk to and from school, and I worry that someone won't be there when they get home. I combat this fear by having two designated places for them to go if they get home and someone is not there. If by some chance those people aren't home, my sons know to go back to school and tell the secretary in the office what has happened. She has several phone numbers to call for them to be picked up. Sure enough, when I was traveling recently, my husband got busy at work and wasn't home when they got there. The alternative plans worked beautifully. Now I know that they will be OK if that ever happens again.
—Mary

ACCEPTING WHAT YOU CAN'T CONTROL

When I was a single parent, my parents used to take care of my kids when I was on a trip. My parents are in their seventies. Whenever I was away, I worried that one of my parents would have a heart attack while they were driving with my children or while they were caring for them. I had feelings of being out of control and fears that my children were not doing well while I was gone. I constantly reassured myself that the odds were with me that nothing would happen to either my kids or my parents. The odds were with me that if an emergency did arise, my kids and my parents were capable of handling it. I had to tell myself that over and over again.

—Jan

You may have identified feelings or situations which have no practical solutions. If you are on a business trip, you simply cannot control whether or not the adult with your children will be caught in traffic and arrive late to pick up your children. You simply must trust them to care for your children and remember the things that need to be done. In short, you have to learn how to "let go" after you walk out the door.

LEARNING HOW TO LET GO

- Develop some self-talk. Make a list of all the reasons you should not be having these feelings of worry. Read through this whenever you are feeling overly concerned. If you are worried, ask yourself what the odds are of your fears being realized. Ask others also. Include this information in your list.

Example: I am worried my parents will have a heart attack while they are taking care of my child.

Self-Talk: My mom is in good health. My father has a weak heart, but he is taking medication and the doctor says he is doing well. Even if my father had a heart attack, my mother would be there to take care of the situation. The chance of them both having a heart attack at the same time is remote!

- Write an affirmation. This is a positive statement which you can recite several or many times a day until you believe it.

Example: My parents love taking care of my children. My children are lucky to spend time with their grandparents. Yes, my parents are old, but they are still capable, responsible people. We are all fortunate to have these circumstances.

- If you are religious, pray. Every day or every time you feel the need, practice handing your feelings over to your higher power.

- Talk with others who experience the same fears/feelings. Ask your friends or co-workers if they feel the same way. Ask them what they do to help alleviate these worries and concerns.

- Symbolically get rid of the feeling. Whenever the feeling becomes intense, write it down on a little slip of paper. Tear up the paper or throw it away and imagine the feeling being destroyed as well.

- If you find that your fears and/or emotions are getting the best of you, by all means, consult a professional counselor, psychologist or psychiatrist.

POSITIVE WAYS TO ACT ON YOUR GUILT AND FEAR

There are also lots of little things you can do to influence how you feel about the job you are doing. Sometimes a string of small positive acts can lead up to a greater sense of control. The following suggestions may help you and your children shed gloomy feelings.

THINKING AND ACTING POSITIVELY

- Ensure that your children are in a safe, loving environment when you are away.

- Put into action one of the solutions you brainstormed in the exercise, **A Process for Working Through Your Feelings**, starting on page 168.

- Put into place one or two of the activities in this book.

- Make a special time or day for your child.

- Send your child a card in the mail telling them how special they are.

- Talk with others in your situation. What do they do? Will it help you to organize an informal support group with them to meet on a regular basis? If it is appropriate, can you include your children?

- Tuck a note in your child's lunch box telling them how much you love them.

- Leave notes around the house in envelopes for your children—one on the couch, one on their bed, one in the toy chest.

10
THE BIG PICTURE

I think if I had to do it over, I would have organized my mornings so that I could have read or sat on the couch and cuddled with my kids for a little bit when they were younger. If we can just step back and smell the roses for even a few moments, that would be a good deal. It's way better than nothing, and they would at least have that memory of the morning.

—Heidi

The key is to find the right balance of work, attention and activities for your family. And while you are using this book to work on that, why not also remind yourself of all the things you are doing as a parent?

TAKING STOCK

- Make a list of all you do for your children. When you look at it, it really adds up, doesn't it!

- Don't compare yourself to other parents and think that you are coming up short. You have different children and different needs as a family.

- The fact that you are using this book shows you are actively trying to do more for your children. How can you complain about that?

- Your working outside the home brings many benefits to your family. List them to remind yourself. (See **Why *Am* I Going to Work?** beginning on page 19.)

- The children of working parents often benefit by learning to be self-reliant at earlier ages. What skills have your children learned because of your work schedule?

- With limited time together, both you and your children have an acute appreciation for the time you do have. Neither of you takes each other for granted.

- You are a role model for your child in two arenas of life: parenting and work.

You have dreams and hopes, and you want everything for your kids. And you want to do everything for them and also do a great job at work. It took me a while to realize that it is okay to buy a pie at the bakery instead of baking it. Finding out that you don't have to be all things to all people helps. Yes, you can do it all, but you just don't have to.

—Candi

As a working parent, you are on both an exciting and challenging path. Concerns about not always being there for your children may surface, but your wisdom and experience from the work place will help you educate and prepare your child for all facets of life.

Children are very resilient. We often don't give them enough credit for "going with the flow." Sure, they like to complain sometimes, but often they are acting just like they did when they were babies—they put up quite a fuss until you walk out the door, then calm themselves and go on their merry way. The important thing is that your children know they are loved.

As long as you approach any problem with love, you can't go wrong. It doesn't matter where you are—your love crosses all distances. So as you and your children continue on your journeys of life, let this book help you spread your love in a few more places as you go. There's no reason to feel guilty about that and every reason to feel proud of the job you are doing as a parent!

APPENDIX A:
COMMUNICATION CENTRAL FORMS

With the following information kept in *Communication Central,* each member of your family will be just a phone call away—and no one will have to search for the number! The forms you fill out depend upon your individual schedules. If any family member has a schedule that changes frequently, make lots of copies of the appropriate form so you will always have spares.

For those of you who work at one central site, fill out **Where I Can Be Reached at Work**. If you or your partner have an irregular schedule, use the worksheet titled **Where I Can Usually Be Reached** to log all the needed phone numbers.

My Activities and Friends can be filled out for each child in your family. It is a handy reference for you, your caregiver and your children. Another essential item for *Communication Central* is an **Authorization for Medical Care**. Make sure to have authorization forms completed, signed and witnessed for each child in your household. Your possible caregivers can each keep an original copy and another one should be kept in *Communication Central.* In an emergency, you'll know that your caregiver can grab the copy in *Communication Central* as they leave to take your child to the doctor or the hospital. Even if your child is at a friend's house, a caregiver can get their form and meet the friend's parent and your child wherever he or she is to receive treatment.

Finally, you will want to have a list of **Emergency Contact Numbers** as well as the instructions for any emergency contact devices you own like a cellular phone or pager. Make sure the adult at home and your children know how your cell phone and your pager work. After you fill out **Cellular Phone Basics** and **Pager Basics**, supervise your children while they practice using them. You may want to post the emergency contact numbers in a prominent place where they are always visible.

WHERE I CAN BE
REACHED AT WORK

by _____

I work at: _____

The central number is: _____

My phone number or extension is: _____

My boss's name is: _____

His/Her phone number is: _____

When I am out of the office, I often can be found at:

_____ Phone: _____

_____ Phone: _____

_____ Phone: _____

I usually eat at:

_____ Phone: _____

_____ Phone: _____

_____ Phone: _____

WHERE I CAN USUALLY BE REACHED

by _____

Cell Phone Number: _____

Pager Number: _____

Routine Activities, Classes or Commitments:

	Activity	Time	Phone
Monday:	_____	____ to ____	_____
	_____	____ to ____	_____
	_____	____ to ____	_____
	_____	____ to ____	_____
Tuesday:	_____	____ to ____	_____
	_____	____ to ____	_____
	_____	____ to ____	_____
	_____	____ to ____	_____
Wednesday:	_____	____ to ____	_____
	_____	____ to ____	_____
	_____	____ to ____	_____
	_____	____ to ____	_____
Thursday:	_____	____ to ____	_____
	_____	____ to ____	_____
	_____	____ to ____	_____
	_____	____ to ____	_____
Friday:	_____	____ to ____	_____
	_____	____ to ____	_____
	_____	____ to ____	_____
	_____	____ to ____	_____
Saturday:	_____	____ to ____	_____
	_____	____ to ____	_____
	_____	____ to ____	_____
	_____	____ to ____	_____
Sunday:	_____	____ to ____	_____
	_____	____ to ____	_____
	_____	____ to ____	_____
	_____	____ to ____	_____

MY ACTIVITIES AND FRIENDS

by _____

School, Preschool or Daycare:

_____ Phone: _____

_____ Phone: _____

I am at: _____ on Monday from _____ to _____

_____ on Tuesday from _____ to _____

_____ on Wednesday from _____ to _____

_____ on Thursday from _____ to _____

_____ on Friday from _____ to _____

_____ on Saturday from _____ to _____

_____ on Sunday from _____ to _____

Activities or Lessons:

Activity	Day	Time		Phone
_____	____	_____	to _____	_____
_____	____	_____	to _____	_____
_____	____	_____	to _____	_____
_____	____	_____	to _____	_____
_____	____	_____	to _____	_____
_____	____	_____	to _____	_____
_____	____	_____	to _____	_____

My Friends:

Name	Address	Phone
_____	_____	_____
_____	_____	_____
_____	_____	_____
_____	_____	_____
_____	_____	_____
_____	_____	_____

AUTHORIZATION FOR MEDICAL CARE

Child's Name: _____ Home Phone: _____

Mother's Name: _____ Day Phone: _____

Father's Name: _____ Day Phone: _____

Doctor's Name: _____ Doctor's Phone: _____

Allergies: _____

Medical Alerts: _____

Blood Type: _____

Insurance Information:

Carrier: _____

Subscriber Number: _____

Carrier: _____

Subscriber Number: _____

I/We give authority to _____ to arrange for
any necessary medical care and treatment for the child named above. The
doctor they contact may provide or obtain medical care for my child which
may include arrangements for the administration of anesthesia and surgery.
The above-named person has the authority to make any decisions necessary
in arranging for appropriate treatment for my child.

Date: _____ Signed: _____
                                                    Mother

Witness: _____ Signed: _____
                                                    Father

EMERGENCY CONTACT NUMBERS

Global Emergency Number: _____

Fire: _____ Poison Control: _____

Police: _____ Pastor/Rabbi/Priest: _____

Ambulance: _____ Family doctor: _____

Pediatrician: _____ OB/Gyn: _____

Hospital: _____ Pharmacy: _____

School: _____ School: _____

Mom's Work: _____ Dad's Work: _____

Dentist: _____ Taxi: _____

Veterinarian: _____ Local Relative: _____

Neighbor: _____ Family Friend: _____

_____ _____

_____ _____

CELLULAR PHONE BASICS

To Make a Call on Our Phone:

1. _____

2. _____

3. _____

4. _____

To Receive a Call on Our Phone:

1. _____

2. _____

3. _____

4. _____

PAGER BASICS

How to Call Me With the Pager

1. _____

2. _____

3. _____

4. _____

How to Receive a Phone Number on the Pager

1. _____

2. _____

3. _____

4. _____

Appendix B:
Profiles of the Voices in This Book

Pati Crofut is a self-employed accountant, adult educator, writer and licensed private pilot. She is a single mom who lives with her two children ages 6 and 11, two cats, a cockatoo and a Bernese Mountain dog. The family spends their winters cross-country skate skiing. In the summer, they can be found most weekends at their remote lake cabin where they get down to the basics of each other and life itself.

Candi English works on the Well Work Team for ARCO Oil Company on the north slope of Alaska. She flies to work for seven days at a time twice a month. Her husband, Stanley, is an Alaskan bush pilot who flies single-engine aircraft on the west coast of Alaska for 20 days each month. They have two children: Molly Marin, 8, and Maile, 2. As a family, they enjoy flying, fishing, camping, and simply having dinner together.

Jeannie Fitzgerald is an at-home mom. Her husband, John Kreilcamp, travels extensively for his job in the tourism industry. They have three children: Hannah, 10, Claire, 8, and Danny, 4. The family enjoys riding bikes and attending the kids' sporting events. John and Jeannie play tennis and their girls have recently joined them on the courts. Jeannie is currently Co-President of her school PTA.

Heidi Hurliman is a nurse practitioner currently working three days a week and pursuing a graduate degree. She and her husband, Kit Coleman, have three children—Henry, 12, Emma, 10, and Charlie, 8. All five of them are making an active effort to survive and thrive in the busy nineties. They all pitch together to run their busy household and jump with even more enthusiasm into family fun.

Rose Kalamarides is the Administrator of employee benefit plans for the Alaska Teamsters, and she travels regularly for her job. She and her husband, Peter, have one child, Molly, 7. They started downhill skiing as a family this winter and Pete and Molly have been taking judo together. Rose plays hockey and reads for relaxation.

Mary Kerr has been in the accounting field for fifteen years. She and her husband, Kevin, have two children—Zachary, 8, and Jacob, 6. After thirteen years of full-time work, Mary changed her work and family balance and started working part-time at her husband's CPA firm. Their family enjoys outdoor activities like camping, fishing and hiking. They are also actively involved in their sons' sports: baseball, swimming, hockey and soccer. Mary assists in her children's classrooms each week and her favorite activities are golf and gardening.

Joanna Knapp has a Master's Degree in Public Management and has been a college instructor, corporate trainer and is now a writer. She and her husband, David, have two children—Alex, 10, and Ian, 4. Joanna and Alex spend time together every week tending injured bald eagles, ravens and songbirds at the Bird Learning and Treatment Center. She and Ian like to read books and take walks. Their favorite family activities are going to their cabin, playing games together, traveling and exploring Alaska.

Richard Kurtz is a licensed marriage and family therapist who maintains a private practice in addition to counseling children for an Alaska Native mental health agency. His wife is a registered nurse in the maternity center of an Anchorage hospital. They have two children, ages 8 and 6, and are expecting a third. Richard and his family enjoy gardening, hiking and skiing, but mostly they just like being with each other.

Doug Nielson is a general contractor with his own construction firm. He lives with his 2 children: Kayli, 11, and Cory, 9. He has one grown stepdaughter and one grandchild; Kodee, age 3. Last year Doug bought a 22-foot sport fishing boat named *Ahaaliq*. He enjoys fishing, beach combing and harbor exploring with his children.

Jan Strait is a flight attendant who can be found in the air between 12 and 17 days a month. She and her husband, David, have a blended family with four children. Three of the kids—Melissa, 12, Alicia, 11, and Brandyn, 9—live with Jan and David, and a daughter, Ashley, 7, resides in Colombia with her mother. Jan grew up in an airline family, so she well understands handling absences from her children. The Straits love to travel and hike. Last year, they visited San Francisco, Mexico, Vancouver Island and Disneyland.

APPENDIX C:
RESOURCES BY CHAPTER

---

2 ANSWERING THE QUESTIONS ALL CHILDREN ASK

BOOKS

Playground Politics—Understanding the Emotional Life of Your School-Age Child by Stanley Greenspan, M.D.

101 Educational Conversations With Your Kindergartner-1st Grader by Vito Perrone—(Also separate books for Grades 2, 3, 4 and 5) This book bridges communication gaps between parent and children. It is designed to help you and your child discuss what he or she is doing in school.

Emotionally Intelligent Parenting by Maurice Elias

Nothing but the Best: Making Day Care Work for You and Your Child by Diane Lusk & Bruce McPherson

Working Fathers: New Strategies for Combining Work and Family by James Levine, Ph.D. & Todd Pittinsky

MAGAZINES

Child
PO Box 5143
Harlan, IO 51593-2643
800-777-0222

Parents
PO Box 3042
Harlan, IO 51537-0207
800-727-3682

Mothering
The Magazine of Natural Family Living
PO Box 1690
Santa Fe, NM 87504
800-984-8116

WEBSITES

www.familiesandworkinst.org
> Website of the Families and Work Institute, a non-profit organization that promotes worksite research on the changing needs of workers with families

www.childcare.ucla.edu/CHILDCARE/wpn.htm
> The website of *The UCLA Working Parents Newsletter*

members.aol.com/zoey455/index.html
> A quarterly on-line newsletter with a feminist slant that chronicles the everyday experience of mothering young children

www.mentor-media.com
> Parenting on the Go website with suggestions for solving behavioral problems of children

www.naturalchild.com
> This website includes parenting advice, letters from readers, a kids' art gallery, and reviews of books and articles on parenting.

3 BUILDING THE LINES OF COMMUNICATION

BOOKS

Games for Writing: Playful Ways to Help Your Child Learn to Write
> by Peggy Kaye

On Line Family—Your Guide to Fun & Discovery in Cyberspace
> by Preston Gralla

Parenting Online—The Best of the Net for Moms & Dads
by Melissa Wolf

*Love Notes to You—A Shared Journal—Parents and Children
Communicating Through Love* by Wendy Holland

Putting Your Heart On Paper
by Henriette Anne Klauser

SOFTWARE

Ultimate Writing and Creativity Center
by The Learning Company (ages 8-12)

E-mail Software
Animated E-mail by Expert

Calendar Software
Calendar Creator by Softkey
Calendar Maker by CE Software
Calendar Shop by Expert

WEBSITES

www.pslivemail.com
Makes it possible for you to create an animated e-mail message
which the recipients can access.

www.postcards.www.media.mit.edu/postcards
Send an electronic postcard to someone you love.

Screensavers
www.customsavers.com
Software that creates screensavers with your favorite images on
them. Purchase the software or download a trial version of it.

Puzzles
www.riddler.com
Crossword puzzles and riddles to amuse the whole family

www.puzzleparlor.com
    A large selection of word and math puzzles for entertainment

Finding Pen Pals
deil.lang.uiuc.edu.exchange
    The Exchange website can help your child find a pen pal. It also
    contains stories written by children all over the world.

www.pen-pal.com
    The Student Letter Exchange website can set your child up with
    a free pen pal.

www.siec.k12.in.us./west/100th/mail.htm
    The E-mail Around the World website can help your child find
    an e-mail pen pal.

CATALOG

W. H. Freeman & Company
41 Madison Avenue
New York, NY 10010
Computer Books for Children

4 CHASING AWAY BOREDOM AND THE BLUES

AUDIO CASSETTE TAPES

Tell Me A Story Tape Book: Eight Stories that Promote Self-Responsibility and High Self-Esteem by Trenna Daniells
Tell Me Some More Stories: Eight Stories that Promote Self-Responsibility and High Self-Esteem by Trenna Daniells

BOOKS

Kids' Party Games & Activities: Hundreds of Exciting Things to Do at Parties for Kids 2-12 by Penny Warner

The New York Times Parent's Guide to the Best Books for Children
by Eden Ross Lipson

MAGAZINES

Family Fun
PO Box 37033
Boone, IO 50037-2033
800-289-4849

The Horn Book Magazine
About Books for Children
11 Beacon Street, Suite 1000
Boston, MA 02108
800-325-1170

SOFTWARE

Fun With Photos
Photosuite by MGI
Power Goo by Kai
Live Pix by Deluxe (Includes photo projects and using photos in e-mail)
Creative Photo Albums by DogByte
Photo Deluxe by Adobe
Picture It by Microsoft

Greeting Cards, Signs, Banners and Craft Software
The Print Shop by Broderbund
Print Artist by Sierra
Printmaster by Mindscape
Print Studio by Micrografx
Greeting Card Maker by Expert

Greeting Cards and Sticker Software for Younger Children
Printertainment by Avery
Print Factory by Crayola
Print Studio by Disney

Games for Boredom
100 Kids' Games by Expert

WEBSITES

Boredom Buster Websites

www.planetoasis.com

> A website with a mock city that you and your children can explore as well as terrific links to many other websites—worth hours of exploration.

bonus.com

> The Kids' Supersite with far too many fun activities to list

www.eduplace.com

> Lots of brain teasers and educational entertainment

www.nj.com/yucky/

> The Yuckiest Site on the Internet should provide your child with some gross-out information and lots of science at the same time.

www.childrensmusic.org

> The website of a non-profit organization dedicated to music for kids

www.lego.com

> A site developed by Lego that includes kids' activities in addition to displays of their products

Bucking the Blues Websites

members.aol.com/depress/children.htm

> A website with information on clinical depression in children

CATALOGS

Hearth Song
Mail Processing Center
6519 N. Galena Road
PO Box 1773
Peoria, IL 61656
Games; Art Supplies

Lilly's Kids
Lillian Vernon Corp.
Virginia Beach, VA 23479
800-285-5555
Games; Activities

Dover Publications, Inc.
31 East 2nd Street
Mineola, NY 11501
Activity Books, Stickers, Coloring Books

5 OUT FOR THE EVENING

AUDIO CASSETTE TAPE

Good Night: Story Visualizations with Sleepytime Music—created and told by Jim Weiss

BOOKS

Keys to Children's Sleep Problems by Susan E. Gottlieb, M.D.

Ending the Homework Hassle by John Rosemond

Homework Without Tears by Lee Canter & Lee Hausner, Ph.D.

SOFTWARE

Cooking Dinner
Complete Interactive Cookbook by Compton's Home Library
Better Homes and Gardens Complete Cooking Suite by Multicom

Homework
There is so much educational software on the market. Look for software developed for your child's age group that focuses on a subject in which he or she is weak.

WEBSITES

Meal-Oriented Websites
www.kidsfood.org
An educational site with information on healthy food choices, hunger in the world, and recipes kids can make themselves

www.roa.com
>   This Recipes of America website has a section called "In Minutes" with recipes for superfast meals.

www.yumyum.com
>   Recipes and a Facts n' Fun area interspersed between ads for products

Homework Help over the Net

member.aol.com/aac4/private/aachomepage/index.htm
>   Homework help for all ages in math, English, history and science

www.shop-utopia.com/reference
>   Homework help as well as a general reference website for a wide variety of information

members.aol.com/jishka/homework_help
>   Help with a broad range of subjects, including foreign languages

CATALOG

Right Start Catalog
Right Start Plaza
5334 Sterling Center Drive
Westlake Village, CA 91361
800-548-8531
Pre-school Games, Videos & Music

6 OFF ON A TRIP

BOOKS

50 Simple Things You Can Do to Raise a Child Who Loves History & Geography by Anne Stribling, M.Ed.

Aunt Dot's Incredible Adventure Atlas by Eljay Yildirim

SOFTWARE

Atlas Software
New Millenium World Atlas by Rand McNally
3D Atlas by Creative Wonders
Atlas of the World by Hammond
Virtual Globe by Microsoft Encarta

Trip Planning Software
Tripmaker by Rand McNally
AAA Map n' Go by DeLorme
3D Explorer USA by DeLorme

Software Companies that Have Software for Learning Individual Languages
The Learning Company   Berlitz
Webster's New World   Syracuse Language Systems
Transparent Language   Triple Play Plus
Knowledge Adventure Jump Start Language Series

Geographical and Exploration Software
Rescue Geo I by Houghton Mifflin Interactive
Amazon Trail, *Africa Trail* and *Maya Quest* by MECC
Where in the USA Is Carmen San Diego? by Broderbund
Where in the World Is Carmen San Diego? by Broderbund

WEBSITES

Travel-Oriented Websites
www.library.advanced.org.10157
Games and a maze by Geo-Globe to test your knowledge about geography

www.travel.epicurious.com
Advice on destinations in all parts of the world

www.travelandleisure.com
Travel information by the folks at *Travel and Leisure Magazine*, including the World's Best Everything list

www.Nationalgeographic.com
Explore the world of National Geographic at their website.

www.exploration.net
Master guide to world travel and destination information with links to other websites

www.traveler.net
Travel website with information on destinations: includes hotels, maps, statistics, weather, time, current events and other websites.

Map Websites
www.maps.com
Sources for maps on-line. Includes an interactive atlas that allows you to view maps, then order them if you want.

mapsonus.com
Navigational maps on-line for the United States. You can enter an address and get a map of the area. If you are traveling in the United States, this site will let your children zoom in on your exact location.

Long Distance Company Websites—Look for plans that will save you money on your long-distance phone bill.
sprint.com
mci.com
att.com

CATALOGS

Hand in Hand Catalogue Center
891 Main Street
Oxford, ME 04270
800-872-9745
Travel Items & Teaching Toys

George F. Cram Co., Inc.
301 S. LaSalle St.
Indianapolis, IN 46201
800-227-4199
Maps, Atlases, Globes

National Geographic Society
1145 17th St., NW
Washington, DC 20036
Travel Aids, Maps, Globes, Books, Games, Videos

7 MANAGING YOUR CHILD'S MEDICAL NEEDS

BOOKS

The Parent's Guide to Baby & Child Medical Care
   edited by Terril H. Hart, M.D.

A Sigh of Relief—The First-Aid Handbook for Childhood Emergencies
   by Martin I. Green

Your Child in the Hospital—A Practical Guide for Parents
   by Nancy Keene & Rachel Prentice

*The Holistic Pediatrician—A Parent's Comprehensive Guide to Safe and
   Effective Therapies for the 25 Most Common Childhood Ailments*
   by Kathi J. Kemper, M.D., M.P.H.

The Penny Whistle Sick-in-Bed Book
   by Meredith Brokaw & Annie Gilbar

SOFTWARE

A.M.A. Family Medical Guide by Dorling Kindersley
The Family Doctor by Creative Multimedia
Home Medical Advisor by The Learning Company
BodyWorks by The Learning Company

WEBSITES

www.medicinenet.com
   General reference medical website; good tips for first-aid resources

www.Kidsdoctor.com

What every parent needs to know to keep their children healthy

www.drsforkids.com

Explains common medical topics concerning children in easy-to-understand language. Includes letters, a topic of the week, and a place where you can ask questions of your own to the pediatrician on the website.

8 MISSING SPECIAL EVENTS, BIRTHDAYS AND HOLIDAYS

BOOKS

Ideas for Families by Phyllis Pellman-Good & Merle Good—More than 1000 ideas for all occasions

New Traditions—Redefining Celebrations for Today's Family by Susan Abel Lieberman

Guilt Free Motherhood—How to Raise Great Kids & Have Fun Doing It by Joni Hilton

SOFTWARE

Click Art: Celebrations and Holidays by Broderbund

Play Creation Software
American Girls Premiere: Create and Produce Your Own Plays by The Learning Company

Story Creation Software
Storybook Weaver by MECC
Paint, Write and Play by The Learning Company
(for younger children)
Orly Draw a Story by Broderbund
Magic Artist by Disney

Music for Little People
PO Box 1720
Lawndale, CA 90260
800-727-2233

Silver Burdett Press
PO Box 2649
Columbus, OH 43216
Holiday Fun

---

9 HARNESSING YOUR EMOTIONS

BOOKS

The Working Woman's Guide to Managing Stress
by J. Robin Powell, Ph.D., C.S.W.

Healing Body, Healthy Woman: Using the Mind/Body Connection to Manage Stress and Take Control of Your Life by Alice Domar

The Artist's Way—A Spiritual Path to Creativity by Julia Cameron

Living the Simple Life—A Guide to Scaling Down & Enjoying More
by Elaine St. James

WEBSITES

www.positiveparenting.com
Resources and information about common parenting problems. Help for making parenting more rewarding

www.mcs.net
Kathy's Essential Information website was created by a terminally ill mother who wanted to impart what she feels is important about parenting to others. This site includes lots of links to other sites.

BOOKS

Living in Balance—A Dynamic Approach for Creating Harmony & Wholeness in a Chaotic World by Joel Levey & Michelle Levey

Fathering—Strengthening Connection With Your Children No Matter Where You Are by Will Glennon

Quantity Time—Moving Beyond the Quality Time Myth by Steffen T. Kraehmer

The Time Bind—When Work Becomes Home & Home Becomes Work by Arlie Russell Hochschild

Stress for Success: The Proven Program for Transforming Stress into Positive Energy at Work by James Loehr

WEBSITES

www.parentsoup.com
A site chock full of information on parenting including resources, fun and games and advice from experts as well as age-specific information

www.momsonline.com
A cyberspace community of moms and dads that offers information, advice, resources and moral support

family.disney.com
Family.Com website with general parenting advice and resources

INDEX

Working Parents **Happy Kids**

ORDER FORM

Quantity	Item	Price	Total
	Working Parents, Happy Kids: Strategies for Staying Connected	$14.95	

Shipping and Handling:		
up to $20.00 .... $3.00	Total of ordered items	
$20.01—$30.00 .. $4.00	Shipping and Handling (see chart)	
$30.01—$40.00 .. $5.00		
more than $40.00 $6.00	TOTAL AMOUNT ENCLOSED	

Name: _____

Address: _____

City: _____ State: _____ Zip: _____

Phone: _____ Fax: _____

E-mail: _____

Please make check or money order payable to **Turnagain Press**.

Turnagain Press
P.O. 240248-B
Anchorage, AK 99524-0248

Orders are shipped via the US Post Office.

THANKS FOR YOUR ORDER!